TRADITIONAL SELF-GOVERNING INSTITUTIONS AMONG THE HILL TRIBES OF NORTH-EAST INDIA

TRADITIONAL SELF-GOVERNING INSTITUTIONS AMONG THE HILL TRIBES OF NORTH-EAST INDIA

Edited by
ATUL GOSWAMI

AKANSHA PUBLISHING HOUSE
New Delhi-110 059 (INDIA)

AKANSHA PUBLISHING HOUSE
R 37-B, Vani Vihar, Uttam Nagar
New Delhi-110 059 Ph.: 5640621
E-Mail: ektabooks@yahoo.com

Traditional Self-Governing Institutions Among the Hill Tribes of North-East India

First Edition, 2002
ISBN-81-87606-24-X

PRINTED IN INDIA

Published by M.P. Misra for Akansha Publishing House, New Delhi and Printed at Mehra Offset Press, Delhi.

Contents

Preface

The book includes eleven papers on the traditional self-governing institutions among the hill tribes of the northeast India, besides an introduction by the editor. With profound knowledge of the numerous tribes inhabiting the hills of the northeastern area, the paper authors not only describe elaborately the institutions, but also critically examine their relevance in the context of the changes taking place in these societies. Researchers on tribal issues are likely to count the contents of the book as fascinating. The book is expected to be rated as absorbing by general readers.

All the eleven papers incorporated in this book, except the one on Manipur, were presented in a workshop organised by the Institute with the financial support from the Rajiv Gandhi Foundation, New Delhi. On behalf of the Institute, I would like to put on record the Institute's deep sense of appreciation to the Foundation for the initiative taken and financial support provided.

I owe a great deal to my colleagues, all of whom showed interest in the publication. I had had fruitful discussions with them before finalising the edited manuscripts. I express my thanks to them. Mr. Rustom Ali, Ms. Pranita Kalita and Ms. Anindita Sharma typed out the finalised manuscripts. They deserve thanks from the editor.

Sri M.P.Misra, proprietor, Akansha Publishing House, New Delhi, also deserves special thanks for bringing out the book.

Guwahati
April 11, 2002

Atul Goswami

List of Contributors

1. B.K. Roy Burman, Professor, Centre for the Study of Developing Societies, New Delhi.
2. J.B. Ganguly, Formerly Vice Chancellor, Tripura University, Agartala.
3. Mahadev Chakravarti, Professor of History, Tripura University, Agartala.
4. P.K. Basu, Department of Political Science, Tripura University, Agartala.
5. A Lanunungsang Ao, School of Agricultural Sciences, NEHU, Mezdiphema, Nagaland.
6. L.B. Thanga IAS (Retd.), Formerly Chief Secretary, Manipur.
7. R.N. Prasad, Professor of Public Administration, NEHU, Mizoram Campus, Aizawl.
8. A.C. Talukdar, Professor of Political Science, Arunachal University, Itanagar.
9. L.S. Gassah, Professor of Political Science, NEHU, Shillong.
10. B.N. Bordoloi, Formerly Director, Assam Institute of Research for Tribals and Scheduled Castes.
11. Amar Yumnam, Professor of Economics Manipur University, Imphal.

Introduction

Present northeast India comprises the States of Arunachal Pradesh, Assam, Manipur, Meghalaya, Nagaland and Tripura covering a geographical area of about 2.56 lakh sq km. It shares more than 4000 km long international land borders with Bhutan, China (Tibet), Myanmar and Bangladesh. This land-locked region is connected with the rest of India through Siliguri in West Bengal by a narrow strip of land of only 20 km width. Its strategic location makes peace and prosperity in the region imperative for national security. Yet, ever since independence, the region has been the hot bed of social turmoil manifested itself in both peaceful agitations and violent group actions (insurgencies and militancies). In order to fulfil the political aspirations of various ethnic groups, a number of new States had to be carved out of the composite Assam during the post-independence period. However, even the creation of these States has not met fully the aspirations of the ethnic groups. There is simmering discontent over a number of issues like large-scale illegal migration across the border, changing the demographic profile of the region; lack of development despite the region's rich resource endowments, which is attributed to the Centre's apathy and neglect accompanied by the incompetence of the State governments. In addition, the social turmoil of the region is reflective of a society in transition, which got exposed only recently, giving rise to conflicts between 'tradition' and 'modernity'. The beneficiaries of some of the decaying traditional institutions are often in clash with the interest of the emerging elite, as the latter are much better placed for deriving the benefits of the modern institutions.

Three valleys (Brahmaputra, Barak and Imphal), surrounded by and interspersed with a number of mountain ranges, constitute the northeastern region. While the valley-dwellers, by and large non-tribals (barring the plains tribals), account for more than seventy per cent of the region's population occupying less than thirty per cent of the geographical area, the hill-dwellers are mostly tribals. The region is a 'museum of nationalities', abode of as many as 130 tribal communities, out of 450 for the country as a whole. The inhospitable hill terrains and difficulties in communications did not deter the British in establishing their suzerainty over the entire region phase-wise.

After annexing the Chittagong Hill Tract from the Nawab of Bengal in 1760, the East India Company assaulted Tripura the very next year with the help of the armed forces of the Nawab. Most of the plains territories of the Tripura king were registered as his *zamindari* while the hills and a patch of plains land were left in the occupation of the king as Independent Tripperah. In 1774, Company forces made a punitive raid on the plains territories of the Jaintia kingdom bordering Sylhet and realized fines from the *raja*. In 1789, the Company intervened in the southern side of the Garo foothills against the oppressive control of the *Chaudhuries* of Mymensingh and some Garo Chiefs entered into a treaty with the Company to be recognized as *zamindars*.[1]

In 1816, David Scot was appointed as the Governor General's Agent to the North East Frontier in addition to his post as joint magistrate of Rangpur and Commissioner of Cooch Behar with the duty of exercising general control and superindence over political relations and intercourse with the petty States including Sikkim, Bhutan, Tibet, Cooch Behar, Bijni, Assam, Cachar, Manipur and Jaintia.[2]

In the Brahmaputra valley, the Ahom monarchy in Upper Assam was tottering under the impact of a series of internecine power struggles from the last quarter of the eighteenth century. The crisis was all-embracing. Ultimately, it gave the Company an opportunity to interfere and project its image as the saviour.[3] In 1792 , the dispossessed Ahom King Gaurinath Singha sought succor from the Company and Lord Cornwallis obliged by sending an expedition to Assam under Captain Welsh. The Mayamoria uprising, which was responsible for outsting Gaurinath, was firmly put down and a commercial treaty struck with the restored king. But with the departure of Welsh, court intrigues and insurrections surfaced once more which led to inviting the Burmese king by viceroy Badan Chandra Barphukan to help restoring order, as the East India Company refused to intervene in his favour. 'Like a mighty rushing wind the Burmese troops reached Assam, took and occupied it with a vengeance. The marauding force stalked the land for several years (1819 to 1824)'.[4] Inspired by easy success in the Brahmaputra valley, the Burmese moved towards Cachar in the south, which was also seriously involved in court intrigues. King Govindachandra sought for assistance from the Company to regain his throne. The Company restored Govindachandra to the throne in 1824 and he entered into a treaty with the Company whereby he put the territory of Cachar under their protection. In 1832 Cachar plain was annexed and its northern hills in two instalments, in 1839 and 1854.

After Cachar, the Company took up operation against the Maans (the Burmese) in the Brahmaputra valley. The atrocious Maans were routed and the Burmese king had to sign the Treaty of Yandabo in 1826, renouncing his claim upon 'the principality of Assam and its dependencies'. Although the Ahom monarchy was restored in 1833 for a brief period, the general administration of Assam was put under the 'Non-regulated system', a system of governance already in operation in the neighbouring district of Rangpur, 'by an executive composed partly of civilians and partly of soldiers upon a mixed system into which the spirit of Regulations is infused in such a way as to cause it to harmonise and blend itself with all that is good in the spirit of native institutions'.[5] This administrative arrangement continued till 31 March 1837. In 1853 district administration was introduced in Assam. On 6 February 1874, Assam became a Chief Commissioner's Province and on 1 September 1905 it because a part of the Lieutenant Governor's Province of East Bengal and Assam. On 1 April 1912, it was separated and converted to Chief Commissionership with a Legislature. In 1921 it became a Governor's Province.

Unlike the valleys, the hills were, by and large, ruled not by kings with well-defined territories, but by Chiefs with three broad types of self-governance: self-regulated convivial type (the Nishis of Arunachal Pradesh), the republican type (more common among the Naga groups of tribes) and the monarchical type (prevalent among the Wanchos of Tirap district, the Khamtis and the Singphos of present Arunachal Pradesh and the Mizo-Kuki Chin tribes). These Chiefs were subjugated by the British in a systematic manner. In 1833 the Khasi Chiefs had to enter into a subordinate alliance with the British and surrendered 31 villages, the administration of which was vested in local heads designated as *Sardars*. In 1854 a junior assistant commissioner was appointed as the administrator of the British portion of Khasi and Jaintia (K & J) Hills. Since 1859 the Khasi Chiefs were required to receive sanads of appointment from the Deputy Commissioner of K & J Hills. In 1835 the Jaintia king was removed and his territory merged with British India. The British K & J Hills district consisted of (a) the hill territories of former Jaintia *raja,* (b) 31 British villages acquired from the Khasi Chiefs and (c) a part of the Shillong town ceded by the Mylliem Siemship. It is to be noted that the Khasi Chiefs, who had formal agreements with the British, signed the instrument of accession at the time of India's independence. In 1869 rules for administration of justice were issued in Garo Hills by the Lieutenant Governor in accordance with the Garo Hills Act of 1869. In 1872 rules for administration of justice and police were issued in Naga Hills, Khasi Hills and Jaintia Hills. The duly recognized village authorities were given the power to try civil and ordinary criminal disputes.

The eastern foothills below the Patkai, inhabited by the Khamptis, Miris, Muttocks and Nagas were subordinated in 1843, when the last batch of recalcitrant Khamptis surrendered. To the west of the region, south of the plains of Nowgóng, lived the Mikirs and behind them the turbulent Rengma Nagas. The former surrendered in 1838, and the latter ten years later. In 1839 a 'forward policy' was initiated in the entire central and western Naga belt. The Lushai expeditions took place in 1871-72 and 1889 after which the hills were brought under British rule.[6]

After subjugating the kings and the Chiefs of the valleys and the hills, the British introduced a number of administrative measures. Those relating to Assam up to 1921 have been already mentioned. The Garos were subjected to Regulation of 1822, while the extension of authority over the Khasi and Cachar hills led to the enactment of Act VI of 1835. The Jaintia territories were divided into twelve dolloiships. The dollois heard all civil cases, at first without exception and after 1841 up to a certain limit, all criminal complaints not of a heinous character in which only the people of their own villages were concerned.[7]

In 1862 Cecil Beadon, the Lieutenant Governor of Bengal laid down that the hill people had to be 'made to understand and feel the power' of the government through a simple plan of government suitable to their present condition and circumstance, and interfering as little as possible with existing institutions' through the extension of intercourse with them and endeavour 'to introduce among them civilization and order'.[8] In 1866 the Lieutenant Governor of Bengal issued two orders constituting the Naga Hills district consisting of that part of the district of Nowgong which lies on the right bank of the river Dhansari, the Naga Hills and the country on both banks of the river Doyang'. In the rules for administrative of justice issued on 1872, the Naga Hills were called an 'agency' and the Deputy Commissioner was renamed ' Political Agent'.[9] The Garo Hills Act (Act XXII) of 1869 defined the boundary of the district. Act of 1835 (insofar as it is related to the Khasi-Jaintia hills) came into force in 1870 and it was extended to the Naga Hills, the Khasi Hills and the Jaintia Hills districts in 1871. The Bengal Eastern Frontier Regulation of 1873 made it lawful 'to prescribe, and from time to time alter by notification a line to be called the Inner Line and to prohibit any subject living outside the area from living or moving therein'. The Inner Line was applicable to the districts of Kamrup, Darrang, Nowgong, Sibsagar, Lakhimpur, Garo Hills, Khasi Hills and Jaintia Hills, Naga Hills, Cachar and Cheettagong Hills. Till 1882 it covered only the Himalayan frontiers and the eastern part of the Naga hills. However, by 1942, when north Cachar was inner lined, all the hills except the Khasi, the Garo and the Mikir were encircled.[10]

Under the Scheduled District Act, 1874, the Lushai Hills were notified in 1898 as a scheduled district, whereby operation of General Laws and Regulations was removed; the same was placed under the superintendence of an officer to be specially appointed for that purpose.

The Assam Frontier Tracts Regulation, 1880 made provision for removal of certain frontier tracts in Assam inhabited or frequented by barbarous or semi-civilised tribes from its operation of enactment in force therein. The Regulation was extended by notification to the districts of the Garo Hills, the Khasi Hills and Jaintia Hills; the Mikir Hills Tracts, the North Cachar Hills, the Sadiya, Balipara and Lakhimpur Frontier Tracts, the Naga Hills district.

The Rules for the Administration of Justice in the Dibrugarh Frontier Tract, 1886 authorised the Political Officer to nominate and appoint the village authorities subject to the confirmation of the Chief Commissioner, and to assign to them their respective functions under these rules. The recognized village authorities were assigned some functions which included policing and administration of criminal and civil justice.

The Assam Frontier Tracts Regulation, 1884 empowered the extension of the Assam Frontier Tracts Regulations, 1880, to certain tracts in Assam. The Regulation was extended to the Garo Hills, Khasi and Jaintia Hills and Nowgong districts.

In 1916 the Indian Penal Code, 1860 was extended to the Sadiya Frontier Tract, Lakhimpur Frontier Tract and the western section of North-east Frontier Tract.

Thus by the end of the British period, administration had spread over all the hills except the areas covered by the Himalayan Frontier Tracts and the so-called Naga Tribal Area.[11]

The Government of India (Excluded and Partially Excluded Areas) Order of 1936 declared the Naga Hills district, the Lushai Hills district, the North Cachar Subdivision of the Cachar district and the North-East Frontier (Sadiya, Balipara and Lakhimpur) Tracts as excluded areas. The Garo Hills district, the Khasi and Jaintia Hills district (excluding Shillong) and the Mikir hill tracts of Nowgong and Sibsagar districts were declared as partially excluded areas.[12]

Chaube succinctly summaries the impact of the British power on the hills. 'The immediate impact of British power on the hills was territorial. When in 1832 Upper Assam was restored to a subordinate monarchy, the prince was granted a limited authority on criminal, and an unlimited authority on civil justice. This pattern was later applied in the administration of the hill areas where the total application of *Pax Britannica* was evidently impossible.'[13]

However, British administration was soon firmly established in the valleys, these being economically more rewarding. The sparsely populated hills with inhospitable terrains were loosely administered through the indigenous social institutions, a device deliberately chosen to gain economic control over the resources at the lowest possible cost. 'The various rules for administration of justice, issued to the districts from time to time, tried to maintain indigenous social institutions while imposing British territorial authority in a more or less uniform way. The application of the rules inevitably created some formalized stereotypes for the administration of the hills, which affected the stability if not the equilibrium of the hill societies traditionally based on unwritten customs. The administration was frequently confronted with peculiar situations. Thus ... the Khasi Siems were turned into some sort of princes in relation to the people, but reduced to petty feudatories under the British government.'[14]

Although the British were in the hills of the northeast for less than a century, they were instrumental in sowing the seeds for transforming the hill societies which were embedded in 'low level equilibrium trap'. Extension of administration necessitated building up small townships deep into the hill areas, construction of pony and cart roads and most importantly, introduction of money, which gradually replaced barter trade, both internal and with neighbouring areas. The two world wars, more particularly the second, fully exposed the hills to the Japanese and the allied forces. Church education acquainted some of them with the rudiments of western ideas and life style. Monetisation led to the emergence of petty traders and business enterprises among the locals. A few from the affluent class went down to neighbouring plains towns of Assam and Bengal for higher education. The outcome of the constellation of factors was the emergence of an embryonic class of persons, the elite, in the hills. If the British administration prepared the ground for social transformation in the hills of the northeast, it was hastened by the Church, which acted as an agency of education and other social services, besides serving as the provider of 'black-coated' occupation. 'The result was the creation of an oligarchy, privileged, salaried and therefore materially powerful section'[15] . Christianity and oligarchy bred individualism particularly in the headquarters towns seeking independence of the Chiefs and freedom from customary communal discipline. Thus 'while it was the policy of the administration to disturb the social equilibrium as little as possible, the challenge posed by the Church went much deeper and upset the traditional power relations. Resistance to such a challenge was natural. However, what is important to note is that the leaders of the resistance were the allies of the government - the Chiefs and officials, the erstwhile champions of vested interest'.[16]

Thus 'though the administration and the Church were functioning in the hills with the same objective, namely the consolidation of British rule, the results were not complementary in all respects. The strategy of the administration was least interference with the existing order, while the activities of the Church tended to undermine its foundation by providing the new elite with intellectual ammunition. The inevitable result was a social imbalance, which not only lingered but also became aggravated after Independence.'[17]

The different types of polity in existence in the region may be summed up as follows:

(i) In Assam, Manipur, Tripura, Cachar and Jaintia Hills there existed monarchies. While the area under Ahom, Cachar and Jaintia kings were merged in the British State of Assam, Manipur, Tripura continued to have their kings under British paramountcy.

(ii) The Khasis, Mizos, Sema and Konyak Nagas etc. had their tribal Chiefs. While there was moderation and dilution of Khasi Siems', powers by the superimposed democratic system, the Mizo Chiefs had perfect autocratic power.

(iii) Most of the tribes had their village tribal councils with different degrees of political, administrative and judicial powers.

(iv) Some tribals, like Angami Nagas followed ultra-democratic norms in running their village and community affairs.[18]

Many of the traditional social and political institutions showed signs of stress under the combined impact of monetization and spread of western education. First, the Chiefs' powers got clipped drastically, although they were allowed to retain some nominal authority. This, in turn, weakened the communal control on land which was fast becoming 'private'. The more or less self-sufficient tribal society was being slowly but surely integrated to the market economy, the traditional indigenous social and political institutions not possessing enough resilience to check the onslaught of the mighty forces of the market. The change was not only irreversible, it was also momentum gaining.

At the time of independence northeast India consisted of (1) the Province of Assam with six Brahmaputra Valley districts (Goalpara, Kamrup, Nowgong, Darrang, Sibsagar and Lakhimpur), two Surma valley districts (Cachar and Sylhet) and three hill districts (Garo Hills, United Khasi and Jaintia Hills and Naga Hills); (2) the North East Frontier Tracts with five frontier tracts (Balipara frontier tract, Abor Hills districts, Mishmi Frontier district, Tirap Frontier and the Naga or Tuensang Frontier Tract) and (3) the princely states of Manipur, Tripura and Khasi states. The predominately Muslim areas of Sylhet district were transferred to East Pakistan (now Bangladesh) at the time of independence, after a referendum. The eight thanas of that district, which form Karimganj district now, were merged with Cachar district.

The post-independence period witnessed massive reorganization of the northeastern States. Manipur, a constitutional monarchy, signed the instrument of merger in 1949. Tripura was the first native State to accede to India. Both became Part C States to start with but subsequently acquired Union Territory status and finally full-fledged Statehood in 1972. The Lushai Hills district of composite Assam finally gave birth to a new State, Mizoram in 1986. Similarly the Naga Hills district of composite Assam became the State of Nagaland (inaugurated in 1964). North East Frontier Agency (NEFA) became the full-fledged State of Arunachal Pradesh (inaugurated in 1987).

The above summary of the political and administrative changes taking place in the northeast since the advent of the British is clearly indicative of the fact that in a highly plural society like that of the northeast, political and administrative accommodation / adjustment has to be made to provide a space for each ethnic group. 'Although many Indians are prone to criticise what they read as failures of the Indian state, a look around the world must compel admiration for India's comparative success in nation-building. Astute political management and constitutional accommodation have harmonised many diversities, despite visible turbulence and confrontation. It would be mistaken to interpret the sharpening of ethnic and other identity differences as spelling disintegration. This is a manifestation of growing political and social consciousness among a heterogeneous but hitherto dormant mass and the competing pulls and pressures this generates. This process has yet to exhaust itself, and nowhere as much as in the northeast'.[19] One should hasten to add that 'the astute political management and constitutional accommodation' mentioned above is as much a legacy of the British rule, as it is the ingenuity of Indian statesmen.

Constitutional provisions were made for ensuring district level autonomy to the tribal areas of the northeast.

Article 244 (2) states that the provisions of the Sixth Schedule shall apply to the administration of the tribal areas in the States of Assam, Meghalaya, Tripura and Mizoram. The tribal areas of the State of Assam include (i) the North Cachar Hills district and (ii) the Karbi Anglong district; of the State of Meghalaya (i) the Khasi Hills district, (ii) the Jaintia Hills district and (iii) the Garo Hills districts; of the State of Tripura, the Tripura Tribal Areas district and of the State of Mizoram (i) the Chakma district (ii) the Mara district and (iii) the Lai district . In addition, by an act of Parliament, the Manipur (Hill Areas) District Councils Act 1971, provides for constituting autonomous district councils in the hill areas of Manipur. The Constitution provides for administration of each autonomous district by a district council consisting of not more than thirty members, of whom not more than four can be nominated by the Governor and the rest elected on the basis of adult suffrage.

The district councils constituted in accordance with the provisions of the Sixth Schedule are conferred legislative, judicial, executive and financial powers which are spelt out in details under the Chapter entitled 'Sixth Schedule' in the Constitution. These districts councils have some appearance of 'states' within a State. However, being autonomous in their internal functioning within the broad constitutional provisions, they differ substantially in laws enacted and rules framed. Even in the matter of voting rights, some autonomous district councils (e.g. the Mara Autonomous District Council of Mizoram) confer the voting right to all eligible adults above the age of eighteen years, while some autonomous district councils lay down additional qualifications for voters like length of stay in the area and right to access to traditional lands (as in the case of Karbi Anglong Autonomous District Council). Again some States have transferred more departments to the autonomous district councils (e.g. the state of Assam) than others. Similarly, the autonomous district councils of different states are subject to varying degrees of control of the State legislatures. Autonomous district councils also differ in matters of decentralization of power to the grass-roots (village) level, setting up of various levels of courts, and in accommodating traditional 'self-governing' institutions to the formal structure.

Noteworthy that although Nagaland and Arunachal Pradesh are tribal hill States, there are no autonomous district councils in these two States. The erstwhile Naga Hills district of composite Assam did not accept the proposal for autonomous district councils. Hence a separate arrangement had to be made in the Constitution for this district. Tuensang had a regional council, which functioned for more than a decade after the formation of Naga Hills Tuensang Area and the State of Nagaland. Later on the regional council of Tuensang was abolished. Instead, the innovative 'village development boards' were introduced in the 1970s by the State government in order to strengthen the traditional institution of village councils.

Arunachal Pradesh became a distinct administrative unit in 1874 as per Regulation 3 of 1873. The administration of the area was vested in the Governor of Assam in accordance with Government of India (Excluded and Partially Excluded Areas) Order, 1936. This arrangement continued till 1947, in which year Indian (Provisional Constitutional) Order 1947 vested the administration of the area in the Government of Assam. Sadiya Frontier Tract was divided into two administrative units in 1948, namely Abor Hills district and the Mishmi Hills district. The plains areas of Balipara Frontier Tract, Tirap Frontier Tract, Abor Hills district and Mishmi Hills district were transferred to Assam in 1951. In 1954, the North East Frontier Areas (Administration) Regulation, 1954 was passed which renamed the North East Frontier Tracts as North East Frontier Agency (NEFA). In 1957, Tuensang Frontier Division was taken out from NEFA and merged with Naga

Hills district to form Naga Hills Tuensang Area. NEFA continued to be without democratic institutions, except for the traditional bodies up to the middle of the sixties of the last century. It had no legislative assembly and Parliament made laws for the Agency. On recommendation by the Erring Committee, the North East Frontier Agency Panchayati Raj Regulation was passed in 1967, providing for a three-tier system of local self-government starting from village through block to district level. [20]

Barring Assam, Manipur and Tripura, the continuation (and increase in the number of) autonomous district councils in Meghalaya and Mizoram even after they had attained statehood appears incongruous as the very purpose of introducing the constitutional institution of autonomous district council to protect the hills people from the domination of plains people of the same State had ceased to exist. However, if perceived as units of self-government, similar to those of panchayats of the plains, the continuation of autonomous district council with some changes even in the hill States has some rationale.

Even if perceived as units of self-government, the autonomous district councils suffer from a number of infirmities, as compared to the panchayats of the post seventy-third amendment period. It may be recalled that inserting a new part, Part IX, in the Constitution, the Constitution (Seventy-third Amendment) Act, 1992 not only widens the democratic base of the Indian polity (by adding to it the third stratum of government below the State level for the rural areas), it also seeks to ensure that unlike in the past, the panchayats constituted in accordance with the provi-sions of the Part function as institutions of self government. The Act provides for constituting panchayats in every State (barring the 'Schedule Areas' and 'Tribal Areas' under the Fifth Scheduled and Sixth Schedule respectively, where provisions of the 1992 Act would not be automatically applicable; its application with any special provisions and modifications would require subsequent legislations) at the village, intermediate and district levels (panchayats at intermediate level may not be constituted in a State having a population not exceeding twenty lakhs). Other mandatory provisions of the Act relate to (i) constituting a gram sabha consisting of persons registered in the electoral rolls of the village., (ii) filling of all seats in a panchayat by persons chosen by direct election from the territorial constituencies, (iii) reservation of seats for Scheduled Castes and Scheduled Tribes proportionate to their respective population in the total population of which not less then one third of the seats be reserved for women, (iv) reservation of not less than one third (including the number of seats reserved for women belonging to Scheduled Castes and Scheduled Tribes) of the total number of seats to be filled by direct election, (v) reservation of the offices of the chairpersons for Scheduled Castes, Scheduled Tribes and women, (vi) fixation of a five-year duration of panchayats, (vii) empowering panchayats to prepare plans for economic development and social justice and implement schemes as may be entrusted to them including those in relations to matters listed in the Eleventh Schedule, (viii) constitution of Finance Commission in every State at a regular interval of five years to review the financial position of the panchayats and (ix) constitution of a State Election Commission in every State for superintendence, direction and control of the preparation of the electoral rolls for, and conduct of, all elections to the panchayats. These mandatory provisions have laid down a solid foundation for democratic decentralization, besides paving the way to the civil society for launching a frontal attack on the forces at present inhibiting the panchayats from becoming vibrant institutions of self-government.

The Sixth Schedule provisions compare unfavorably to those of the (Seventy-third Amendment) Act, 1992 on a number of points. In the Sixth Schedule there are no mandatory provisions for (i) reservation of seats for women and reservation of offices for women members, (ii) establishing a quinquennial finance commission for looking after the financial health of the councils, (iii) constituting bodies below the district level with clear demarcation of functions and power, (iv) reserving seats for minority social groups proportionate to their respective population in the total population, (v) empowering the councils to prepare plans for economic development with social justice and (vi) holding of elections within a period of not exceeding six months in the event of dissolution of the councils. The positive elements of the Seventy-third Amendment Act need to be emulated by the autonomous district councils. There is no constitutional hurdle in doing this. Article 243 (4) (a) provides that the Legislature of a State referred to in Sub-clause (a) of Clause (2) (viz the States of Nagaland, Meghalaya and Mizoram) may by law, extend Part IX to the State, if the Legislative Assembly of the State passes a resolution to that effect by a majority of the total membership of that house and a majority of not less than two-thirds of the members of the house present and voting. It is to be added that the power of the district councils in matter of administration of justice is handicapped by the rule making power of the Governor. Similarly the law making power of the district council is of limited operational value, as laws, promulgated by the council until assented to by the Governor can have no effect.

If the traditional 'self-governing' institutions of the hills of the northeast showed signs of stress under the combined impact of monetisation and spread of western education during the British rule (by giving birth to a small section of the privileged class, whose interest clashed with that of the incumbents of the traditional order), the strain got heightened by the constitutional provisions of the Sixth Schedule. The constitutional bodies of autonomous district councils had the effect of intruding into the functional domain of the traditional bodies, in many cases superseding the latter. Thus, in Mizoram, immediately after their constitution, two autonomous district councils abolished the traditional dues payable to the Chiefs in 1953 through necessary enactment. Further the Mizo Districts Council persuaded the Government of Assam to abolish chieftainship. Accordingly, the Assam Lushai Hill District (Acquisition of Chiefs' Rights) Act 1954 abolished the autocratic institution of chieftainship in Mizoram in areas falling under the jurisdiction of Mizo Hills District Council and the Pawi-Lakher Regional Council. All the autonomous district councils constituted in accordance with the provisions of the Sixth Schedule were empowered to make laws relating to, among others, appointment or succession of Chiefs. Consequently, like the Khasi Siems, all Chiefs in areas falling under the jurisdiction of autonomous district councils became subordinate officials of district councils. This further strained the relationship between the district councils and the traditional institutions. This strained relationship between the statutory and traditional bodies is observable in Arunachal Pradesh also where the statutory bodies happen to be panchayats. Even the Kebang (traditional village councils of Adi group of tribes of Arunachal Pradesh) proceedings are being increasingly dominated by elected panchayat members, despite their inadequate knowledge of customary laws. Nagaland is probably the only State where the clash between the statutory and traditional institutions at the village level has not surfaced as the statutory institution of the village council has incorporated in it the essence of the traditional system.

Despite the absence of democratic norms in most cases, the traditional institutions still continue to receive substantial popular support. It is the traditional institutions which do the back-seat driving in case of confrontation with the state and state apparatus. Similarly, in the regulation of basic institutions centring family, property and customary matters the traditional village headman and his associates play important roles. The most serious infirmity of traditional institutions is the absence of women participation in their working. It is a paradox that even though women participate in productive activities very intensely, they have no place in the decision-making process. Therefore, in trying to accommodate some of the traditional institutions to the statutory bodies care has to be taken to see that these traditional institutions do not deny the legitimate democratic rights to any section of their contemporary society.

References

1. S. K. Chaube, *Hill Politics in Northeast India*, Orient Longman, Patna, 1999, p. 3.
2. *ibid.*
3. Rajen Saikia, *Social and Economic History of Assam*, Manohar, 2000, New Delhi, p. 11.
4. *ibid.*, p. 12.
5. H. K. Barpujari, *Assam in the Days of the Company*, North Eastern Hill University Publications, Shillong, 1996, p. 22.
6. S. K. Chaube, *Hill Politics in North East India*, op. cit., pp. 7-8.
7. *ibid.*, p. 12.
8. Alexander Mackenzie, *History of the Relations of the Government with the Hills Tribes of North East Frontier of Bengal*, Quoted by S. K. Chaube, *ibid.*, p. 13.
9. *ibid.*
10. *ibid.*, pp. 14-15.
11. *ibid.*, p. 16.
12. *ibid.*, pp 23-24.
13. *ibid.*, p. 37.
14. *ibid.*, p. 57.
15. *ibid.*, p. 63.
16. *ibid.*, p. 64.

17. *ibid.*, pp. 65.

18. B.B. Kumar, *Reorganization of North-East India*, Omsons Publications, New Delhi, 1996, p. 3.

19. B.G. Verghese, *India's North East Regurgent*, Konark Publication Pvt. Ltd., New Delhi, 1996, pp. xii - xiii.

20. B.B. Kumar, *Reorganization of North-East India*, op. cit., p. 49.

1

Traditional Self-Governing Institutions Among the Hill Tribal Population Groups of North East India

– *B.K. Roy Burman*

At the outset the concept 'traditional' or 'tradition' requires to be examined in some detail. The other concepts which require some probe at least in passing are "self-government" and "hill tribal population".

Tradition as Adaptive Continuity

Generally two dimensions are associated with tradition: temporal and ethical. Action pattern accepted by the concerned group which is time honoured and is transmitted from generation to generation through socialisation process respected by the group comes under the rubric tradition. There is also an ethical dimension in tradition. Breach of tradition is considered to be unethical. It is the ethical dimension which marks out tradition from convention. Deviation from convention may weaken the individual's link with the concerned group; the individual may suffer 'loss of face', but the individual's action as such may not be considered as immoral. In actual life the distinction may not be so sharp, but it would be useful to differentiate between tradition and convention. Without ranking them, it would be good to keep in mind that there is no society which is neither tradition bound, nor convention bound.

Interlacing of temporal and ethical dimensions and the social acceptance of the same imparts elements of dynamism and change to tradition. In response to new challenges or to the emergence of new needs of the society there may be changes in the permutation and combination of the three dimensions of tradition and there may be time gap in varying degrees in their harmonizing with one another. Hence tradition and traditional behaviour pattern should not be considered to be immutable facets of social living. Change is the legitimate offspring of tradition.

An illustration will clarify the meaning of this statement. Most of the Rongmei Nagas of the village Awangkhul in Manipur have been Christians for three generations. They have vast tract of forest land at their disposal. In 1979 they delineated about 5000 acres of land for community horticulture and forestry. First they started with the plantation of a community orange orchard. This was a new mode of production. So long they had been regulating access and use of the sources of production; they had also been collectively helping individual households in the productive activities in case of necessity. But this was the first time they had gone for collective production for sharing the collective output according to norms laid down by the collectivity.

When they were to start their plantation, the whole village gathered at the spot. The seniormost person of the founder clan of the village brought out the gong and other paraphernalia which about 40 years ago they had used, for invoking the blessings of their deities in Rongmei pantheon, for the success of their cultivation. The villagers stood in two rows - one headed by the village headman, and the other headed by the chairman of a non-official activist organisation set up by the villagers themselves. The seniormost member of the founder clan started chanting and making body movements as he would have done before being converted to Christianity. The whole village joined him in chanting but neither the old man nor the villagers invoked the ancient deities - being Christians they could not do it. They invoked the ancestors of the different clans.

The aura of tradition was there; but what they did was not a carbon copy of the chanting and invocation their ancestors or some of the surviving old persons did for the last time forty years ago.

In the pre-conversion days while led by the seniormost elder of the founder clan, the elders of the other clans carried on invocating chants for the blessings of the tribal deities, the other members of the community would go on dancing to the rhythm of the gong. They would not stand in rows as they do in the church during the Sunday prayer. Also there was no voluntary activist association, outside the kinship framework, whose head was to be given a special position. But they had a tradition of honouring persons who did something specially good on critical occasions of the community.

While, what the Rongmeis of Awangkhul did in 1979, was not the exact replica of what they would have done one or two generations ago, some of the behavioural aspects which they considered in 1979 to be the core of the tradition, were repeated. The seniormost member of the founder clan who otherwise was not an influential person in the village at the time of re-enacting the past, was assigned his traditional role; the gong and other ritual paraphernalia which had not been used for forty years were used in the way they were used in the past, with the same sense of solemnity, perhaps with different degrees of intensity. Along with the tribal deities, the ancestors were invoked in the past; on this occasion also the ancestors were invoked. The obliteration of the supernatural deities and the deification of the ancestors alone, was perhaps a subtle shift from the uncanny shadow of the unknown to the loving smile of the known. The moral sanction for the new mode of production, as some would be inclined to conceptualise in political economic term, flew out of it. Even for the special role assigned to the chairman of the voluntary association, a less frequently occurring tradition could be referred to. While standing in rows and everyone participating in the invocative chant was a departure from the pre-existing tradition; it was part of a parallel tradition in the making. For two generations they had been behaving like this in the church on solemn occasions. It had been a time honoured practice. Though it had been a different type of behaviour; the spirit behind it was the same as the earlier form of behaviour. The earlier form of behaviour was an expression of the solidarity of the village community; the new form of behaviour also carried the same meaning. Departure in some forms of action, was not seen as a violation, but as reinforcement of the tradition through adaptation to the new situation.

There is another side of the legitimisation of new mode of production by invoking selective elements of the tradition. There is a hiatus in the *de jure* right and *de facto* right in respect of the forest tracts under the disposal of the Rongmei Nagas. While the *de jure* right over the forest tract belongs to the state, the *de facto* right claimed by the community is that the tract belongs to it. By reviving the traditional practice with requisite adaptive changes, the village community not only reinforced its solidarity but also established customary right over the forest tract. As it turned out later, by this shrewd move the village community could thwart the attempt of the state forest department to take over the forest under cover of development.

This brings into focus the context or the motivation for adaptive change in tradition or traditional behaviour. At this stage, this aspect need not be gone into further. The purpose of narrating the event at Awangkhul is to illustrate the point that tradition is sustained through adaptive changes. Hence a study of persistence or apparent disappearance of traditional self-governing institutions is also a study of change and/or suspended animation of self-governing institutions. More frequently than not, tradition does not die; it may change its form through accretion or demition or otherwise; it may drop or acquire new ancillaries; it may even maintain the form but change the meaning – but in all cases the effective-ethical dimension associated with it tends to persist. All these will be illustrated with reference to the self-governing institutions in North East India. But before doing that the concepts 'self-government' and 'hill tribal population' will be discussed in a summary manner.

Self Government

There is a general impression that pre-colonial Indian villages were isolated, self-governing little republics having nearly everything that they can want within themselves, and almost independent of any foreign relations. They seem to last where nothing else lasts. Dynasty after dynasty tumbles down, revolution succeeds revolution – but the village community remains the same (*Metcalfe's Minutes on the Settlement in Western Provinces, 7th November, 1830*). In case of the tribal communities the picture of isolation is even more complete.

A few decades ago Roy Burman drew attention to the fact that the tribal communities generally existed in contact zones of two or more dominant politico-cultural entities and that frequently they played bridge or buffer roles in between the dominant entities. He rejected the stereotype of isolation in respect of the tribal communities. Of late social historians are questioning the image of isolated republic in respect of Indian villages also (Steward Gordon 1994 : *Marathas, Maraudars and State Formation*; Oxford University Press Delhi, p. 100). He finds considerable peasant mobility with villagers as active negotiators in the larger political processes of the eighteenth century. In a UNESCO publication, Roy Burman referred to the same process among the tribals of Chotanagpur (*Post Primitives in Chotanagpur; Trends in Ethnic Group Relations in Asia and Oceania*, 1979). While rejecting the myth of isolation, one must not swing to the other extreme of denying the prevalence of considerable self-governance, particularly among the tribal communities. The question is whether this self-governance is/was complete in all spheres complemented by articulation with the wider polity. In the latter case, awareness of the nature of wider articulation becomes a part of the study of traditional self government among the tribal communities.

In recent years the question of self-government of the tribal peoples has been mixed up in international parlance with self-determination. In 1966, the UN had adopted two covenants on human rights, namely, International Covenant on Economic, Social and Cultural Rights and International Covenant on Civil and Political Rights. Article 1, para 1 of both the covenants stipulates "All peoples have the right of self-determination. By virtue of that right they freely determine their political status and freely pursue their economic, social and cultural development". At the stage of deliberation on the two covenants, India lent its support to the inclusion of the term "right of self-determination" and India's representative stated in the UN forum that it was inherent in a true democracy. Later India ratified the two covenants. Of direct relevance to the tribal communities is the draft declaration by the UN Working Group on Indigenous Populations. Though the term 'indigenous' cannot be exclusively used for the tribal peoples in India or Asia, international agencies and large sections of tribal intelligentsia in the country have tended to accept the equation, perhaps because in another international document, namely, ILO Convention 107 of 1957 "indigenous" and "tribal" were clubbed together and India had ratified the Convention. A discourse on self-government of the tribal peoples would therefore be incomplete if the concept of self-determination is not addressed to. Many eminent jurists dealing with international law expressed the view that under UN Charter right of self-determination does not imply right of secession. The UN is the creation of independent states and they cannot give mandate to the UN to do anything to dismantle the states except for promoting independence of non-self-governing trust territories. The position was clearly stated by the Secretary General of UN in 1970 to the effect that right of self-determination under UN system does not and cannot include right of secession. Even then two Committees set up by UN forums – one headed by Gross, the other by Crestescu, examined the matter and ruled out right of secession as a part of self determination within the UN framework.

With this clarification, the structure and process of traditional self-government vis-à-vis those of self-determination require to be considered. Though both self-government and self-determination may cover the same interest areas, there is a basic difference between the two. In case of self-government the moral binding within the community is the primary motive force; in case of self-determination it is the power dimension – internal and external to the social processes of concerned people which is more prominent. It does not mean that in self-determination, moral binding does not play any role. But it is more of an instrumental role, complementary to several other factors and processes. Looked in a different way, in self-government moral binding is an end in itself; it represents an act of self-immersion of individuals in the sublime psychic depth of the collective oneness; self-determination on the other hand is almost a continuous process of discovery of untrodded territories in different realms of life and of assertion of right of managing and shaping the same through hegemonic domination of a particular segment of the collectively or through coalition of fractional interests of the collectivity, if necessary.

Self-government of any entity is also to be differentiated from local self-government of the same entity. As already mentioned, self-government is almost *sui generis* in character. Even though it might have a history, it transcends history; it becomes meta-historical. It is inherently autonomous; or through a process of becoming it acquires the attributes of autonomy. Local self-government on the other hand, has hardly any real autonomy. It derives its legitimacy primarily from extra-local authority. But over the length of time the extra-local authority may turn into a nominalistic fiction and the institution of local self-government may emerge as the institution of self-government. The local withers away and the cosmos is born. In this perspective tradition does not always bear the testimony of the past. One can look for it in the promise of the future. But then the moot question is : promise for whom? This leads to the third conceptual issue mentioned earlier.

Population vs. Peoples vs. People

Population means an ensemble of persons, not necessarily with a structural relationship among themselves. For the term people, there is no universally accepted definition. But it is not just an assemblage of persons; it is a collectivity with a sense of identity. Peoples again is not an assemblage, of which 'people' constitute the component unit. Peoples are distinct socially, culturally and otherwise structured entities, which over a length of time may turn into a single people through participating in common endeavours. It is difficult to say that all the tribal communities in India or even in North East India have forged a common identity and emerged as a single people. They are also not amorphous populations; they are peoples. The central concern of the present paper is a rapid probe of the institution of self-government of the tribal peoples. The aspects covered here are (a) broad over-view of the historical ecology of North East India, (b) structural arrangements for self-government and behavioural pattern of the concerned peoples, (c) sources of legitimisation of the structural arrangements, (d) areas of action, (e) operational processes, (f) linkages with state apparatuses, and states processes and regulatory institutions in the region, (g) ramifications on social, political and economic processes of the wider society.

Broad Overview of Historical Ecology of North East India

North East India is the meeting point of four subcontinents, namely, South Asia, South East Asia, East Asia and through Tibet, Central Asia. Pastoral economy was the dominant source of livelihood; long distance trade connecting various parts of Asia with one another and with Europe was ancillary to this. The dominant source of livelihood in South Asia, South East Asia and East Asia was agriculture. Ancillary to the same were handicrafts, animal husbandry, collection and consumption of forest products and long and short distance trade. Symbiotic relations between Central Asia and other regions were more, than those between the other regions, as their dominant sources of livelihood were more or less the same. Long distance trade through land route in pre-colonial period promoted the existence of bridge and buffer peoples with politico-cultural cores and capacity to accommodate institutional attributes and traits from other cultures through a process of syncretism, continuous reinterpretation of the reality and with a sense of collective custodial responsibility about the surroundings. Most of the social formations playing bridge and buffer roles can be categorised as tribal peoples.

With the establishment of hegemonic Mongol control of the regions through which the inter-continental trade routes passed, as a sequel to Zengish Khan's avalanche-like march of conquest and penetration of Mongol dominance upto Yunnan in China within a generation after him, the chain of alliance and hostility balancing each other was disrupted. Large scale South, South East and South

West-ward migration of tribal and peoples analogous to tribal social formations took place during the 13th and 14th centuries AD. Some of the migrant peoples reached North East India.

Again with the growing importance of international marine trade another disruption took place. Long distance land trade route became slender in volume. While short and medium distance land route trade gained ground, the direction of the trade changed. Commodities had to move towards entreports. To ensure this, kingdoms and mercantile establishments backed by the armed might of the sponsoring kingdoms and states in Europe became operative in various forms during the 17th and 18th centuries. In the wake of this, the inter-peoples relations which came up during the 13th to 17th centuries were again put to strain and spurt of migratory movements took place during the 18th and 19th centuries. Bulk of the Mizo-Kuki Chin group of tribes, as well as the Khamtis, the Singphos and their agnates migrated to different parts of North East India during this period. These contingent facts of history had their bearing on the traditional self-government of the tribal communities.

During the colonial period contradiction of the strategic interest of the empire and the commercial interest of the establishment was an important fact to shape the British policy towards the tribal peoples.

In independent India, growing articulation of the state process with the neo-colonial world-order dominated by capitalist technocratic-bureaucratic nexus smothered by particularistic human right orientation, rooted in European history, and the ethos of India's own freedom struggle has been the most important factor in guiding the tribal policy through twists and turns. The various dimensions of tribal self-government in North East India are to be understood in this context as well as the context of ecological constraint related to the interplay of various factors and processes.

Structural Arrangement for Self-government and Behaviour Pattern of the Concerned Peoples

Broadly three types of self-government are found among the tribal communities of North East India. They are: self-regulated convivial type, republican type and monarchical type – each with a transformational potential over a length of time. Each of these types may have the attributes of a regime with subjugated social formations under its shadow; again each of these types may be under the shadow of a regime with stronger power base. In each case the density of the shadow may not be uniform; may even be porous. Again in between each of these types there may be intermediate structures or structural designs. Again transcending its limit, each of these types may move for meta-structural design and may either succeed to build it up or may recede, when faced with adverse factors and processes. Self-regulated convivial type is represented by the Nishis. Traditionally they do not have village level or supra-village level organisation. Their habitat tended to be scattered long-houses, each of these house having a number of households, generally bound together by having a common ancestor. Intra-longhouse disputes were generally settled by the seniormost male member of the longhouse. In case of disputes between members of two long houses help of a mediator selected through the process of divination would be obtained. If necessary the mediator would ask for the assistance of influential elders in the neighbourhood.

In Weberian term Nishi social formation may also be described as 'regulated anarchy'. But this 'anarchy' had also the character of a collective regency. The Sulungs, a neighbouring tribe, were like serfs and had to render free labour for stipulated number of days. The Sulungs had their traditional village councils which exercised considerable control over the members on matters concerning the basic institutions of marriage, succession, sharing of the common land-based resources. But they had to put up with the intervention of the Nishis.

It is difficult to say that the Nishis were under a dense political shadow of any regime in the pre-British period. But as they used to serve as middlemen between the Apatanis, who had developed sophisticated agricultural technology and the peoples in the plains, they had to be in good terms with both. The Nishis near the foothills had from time to time agreed to pay ceremonial homage or even political tribute to the Ahom kings and on some crucial occasions they helped Ahom kings to fight their adversaries. It may be said that at least some sections of the Nishis were under porous political shadow of Ahom kingdom. But the institutional arrangement through which the relationship was regulated is not clear, in view of the fact that the Nishis did not have even village level government.

The republican type of institutional arrangement was more common and is still more common among the tribal peoples of North East India. Particularly among the Naga group of tribes, republicanism had an aura of ideology, which is its turn was related to the pattern of control and management of land and land based resources. But it would be incorrect to say that all Naga tribes were republican in orientation. For example, in Manipur, the Mao Nagas were having hereditary Chiefs.

The monarchical type, with ranking system veering towards stratification system is best exemplified among the Wanchos of Tirap district in Arunachal. The Wancho people are divided into four ranked collectivities (The system may not be called stratification system as there is hardly any difference in life-style except in ceremonial matters). At the top are the nobles; at the bottom are the commoners; in between the two are persons involved in mixed marriages and their descendants. The Great Ang of Mon has a number of villages under him, not only in Arunachal Pradesh but even in Burma who pay tribute to him.

The monarchical type operates among the Khamtis, the Singphos, the Mizo-Kuki Chin tribes along with many others. The Khasi Chiefs (Syiems) had also formal agreements with the British and at the time of India's independence they signed the instrument of accession. Tripura was a full fledged prince's state and the Tripuri king belonged to a tribal people.

Though in structural arrangement there was considerable similarity, the historical process of emergence of this type of institution was not same. Three broad processes can however be noted. The role of the Khasi Chiefs was related to the maintenance of long distance trade connecting the plains south of the Khasi and Jaintia Hills with Brahmaputra valley and beyond. The Syiem was more of a spokesman of the community than a ruler. His role was reinforced by the association of an oligarchy; but in the access to the productive resources the commoners also had a right to a fair share.

Origin of Tripuri kingdom also seems to be related to long distance trade connecting the hill tract in the south with the plains of Bengal. More than internal factors, the external support of the Sultanate of Gour seems to have provided advantage to the Tripuri Chief over the rivals, particularly of Riang tribe for ascending the throne. Tripuri kingdom could not therefore take the character of an absolutist state. It was an internally segmented polity and considerable autonomy was exercised by the tribal social formations. Except for the Mizo-Kuki group of tribes (who had settled in the north east of Tripura, and had Chiefs who were looked upon by their peoples as king, under the King of Tripura, whose title in their language was something like an emperor), other tribes had headmen, assistant and council of elders at the village level.

The monarchical type of self-government among the Mizo-Kuki group of tribes, and perhaps among the Singphos, the Khamtis can be related more to inter-tribal feuds, conquests and to the fact of being subjected to a state of almost perpetual instability for several centuries. As mentioned earlier two stage disruption of inter community socio-political arrangements in Central and East Asia in the middle ages had caused mutual jostlings and pushing and migratory movements on a continental scale. In these periods of perpetual flux, autocratic leadership had emerged among the peoples concerned. They were rulers of their subjects, rather than owners of territories. Territory provided the nexus for the sustenance of the social organisation, but not the core around which the social organisation was woven. This comes out from two facts. First, among the Mizos, if a person killed an animal in the territory of another Chief, he had to give flesh tribute to his own Chief and not to the Chief in whose territory the game was bagged. Second, during war, the Chief depended on a hero, called pethe, who enjoyed many privileges in the community life. But in the matter of management of land he had to depend on a council of elders, called Upas, selected by him from among the different lineages. There are documents which indicate that the colonial rulers in their interest tried to enhance the role of the Chief, and projected him almost like a landlord. But there was widespread resentment against this among a large section of people. Though for sometime after independence, the Government tried to protect the position of the Chief, the people's mobilisation forced the Assam Government to pass an Act in 1954 based on a resolution adopted by the Lushai Hill Autonomous District Council to abolish chiefship. Elected village councils were established, but subsequent events suggest that the structural arrangement adopted as a replacement of autocratic chiefship was not adequate to meet all facets of the situation.

One aspect of Mizo-Kuki chiefship deserves special mention. It was noted by Soppit decades ago, that where the Kukis had been living peaceful life for a ling time, the autocratic character of chiefship tended to be eroded and a more democratic pattern came to prevail. Frequently the

Mizo-Kukis describe the Chiefs as custodians of their interests, but as already indicated, there was vested interest to project the role of custodians and spokesmen as that of rulers. It will be shown later that there is also a vested interest to project their roles as custodians as that of owners of the resources.

Inter-relationship Among the Three Broad Patterns of Structural Arrangements

The inter-relationship can be examined in terms of different analytical frameworks. One is the framework of eco-institutional dynamics; the other is the positivistic framework of empiricism.

The framework of eco-institutional dynamics presented here is a radical departure from the conventional system of classification of societies. In the conventional system, societies are classified with reference to the main economic activity. Thus they are classified as hunters and gatherers, shifting cultivators, settled agriculturists, livestock rearers, craftsmen and traders, dependent on industrial technology, multi-dimensional post-industrial explorers of new society.

The framework of eco-institutional dynamics defines social formation with reference to locus in two axes; one is physical environment-human relationship, the other is inter-human relationship.

Primal hunting and gathering peoples were dependent on ingratiating mode of subsistence and lived on convivial social relationship; similarly early slash and burn agriculturist peoples depended on convivial-ingratiating mode of production; the settled agriculturists were having convivial custodial mode of production, the peasants involved in market economy moved towards convivial-predatory mode of production, the colonial industrial societies generated predatory saptral mode of production and today when existence of life on the planet has obviously become problematic, the highly industrialised peoples are pushing ahead a predatory-demiurgic mode of production.

This ideal typical eco-institutional framework is not however always an empirical reality. One of the reasons is that though today the existence of life on the planet is generally perceived to be problematic, there is no reason to think that similar perceptions were not there, when any particular mode of subsistence or of production passed through a period of crisis due to natural calamity, longterm climatic change reaching a turning point, mismatch between population growth and subsistence base and such other causes. On all such occasions the linkage between nature-human relationship and inter-human collective relationship would be put to severe strain and may experience schizophrenic break of the linkage. In such cases permutation and re-combination may take place and bits of one type of relationship may be linked up with bits of another type of relationship. It would therefore be unpredictable intervention of history rather than predictable operation of social law. This is a possibility which should not be ruled out. But admittedly hardly any work has been done on this line.

With positivistic orientation, based on his experience in Manipur R.K. Das suggests that authoritarian chiefship among the tribal communities is assailed from two directions, namely confrontation with polity with stronger power-base and aspirations and political assertion of commoners. Through combination of these two processes, the authoritarian chiefship tends to give place to republical polity. There is considerable logic and empirical support for this position. But two other possibilities should also be kept in view. Regimes with stronger power-base may promote authoritarian chiefship as a policy of subsidiary alliance. Kabui referred to this in respect of some sections of the Anala. Again, to avoid mutual confrontation, the authoritarian Chiefs may promote republical polity as a territorial buffer or a functional buffer.

Sources of Legitimisation of Structural Arrangement

Srivastav observed ontological root of Chief's power among the Wanchos. The Chief is sacred, so is his blood. Chief's successors also must be of pure blood.

Role of external agencies to redefine the tradition and to influence the traditional structural arrangements has received some attention of ethnographers. Perhaps more analytical appraisal is needed. One illustration would be provided here by referring to the Toto, a small tribe in the border of Bhutan and West Bengal. In the pre-British period the Toto village had changed hand several times between Koch kingdom and Bhutan. Ultimately Bhutan firmly established its control. Each Toto clan had its delineated area in the village for slash and burn cultivation. The Totos had a dual division - one division involved in carrying on trade in Koch kingdom and bringing articles needed by the Bhutias at Totopara; the other division was engaged in carrying the articles needed by Bhutias from Totopara to Bhutan and on return journey carrying commodities needed by the people of the south. By this arrangement, even when Bhutan and Koch kingdom were at war the flow of commodities remained undisturbed. Each division had a headman. When in 1865 the British took over Totopara, in the wake of Anglo-Bhutan war, the Chief of the southern division had to negotiate with the new rulers on behalf of the entire Toto people. He thus emerged as the head of the village as a whole. The Chief of the north division however was not completely divested of his position. Totos were culturally closer to the Bhutias, and the Chief used to monitor the observance of the matters related to culture and custom. With loss of his secular role, he now emerged as the custodian of the religion of the people.

Another interesting change took place. Bhutan had lost its political control of Totopara, not through political assertion of the Totos but through external intervention.

The Governor of Bhutan at Paro lost his coercive power, but did not lose his image as ultimate authority in social matters. A dissociation of authority and power took place. Till the late 50's of the last century, the Totos continued to pay tribute to him. But there was a change in the perception about the nature of the tribute. Earlier it was payment to the ruler; in the changed context it acquired a sacerdoral character and became ritual offering to the authority on religio-cultural matters. The priest headman used to perform a rite with the sacrifice of a pig and a fowl at the time of making the payment. This was a case of a secular power turning into a sacred authority.

Similar process seems to have taken place in parts of Kameng district of Arunachal. But the descriptive accounts are not adequate for coming to definite conclusion.

Role of the king/state as a source of legitimisation of structural arrangement cannot be ignored. Among all the tribes of Tripura while the village headman was selected by the villagers (and while generally the son succeeded the father) confirmation by the king was necessary. During the British rule in the administered areas of Arunachal, Nagaland and in the partially excluded areas of Nowgong, Sibsagar, Cachar (which are now mostly included in the Sixth Schedule areas of the state) the Gaonburhas selected by the villagers required government confirmation. In all such cases there was a mix of endogenous process and the potential of exogenous intervention, which however was rarely exercised contrary to the endogenous process. On the other hand, the fact that the endogenous process took place in the shadow of potential exogenous intervention could not but influence the endogenous process itself. Over a length of time the structural arrangement tended to be considered by the concerned peoples as a part of their tradition of self-government, whereas the state looked upon it as institutional arrangement for local self-government. This hiatus in perception is of considerable importance.

Though the prevailing structural arrangements are not exactly rooted in tradition this have acquired the aura of tradition and introduction of any alternative structural arrangement is looked upon by the concerned people as intervention in their tradition; but in view of the fact that even in the prevailing structural arrangement the state has a role, the policy makers of the state do not consider it an imposition if an alternative structural arrangement is introduced.

Pragmatism in Interpreting Structural Arrangement of Self-government

In 1974, the Autonomous District Council of Tengnoupal district of Manipur constituted a committee with the present writer as Chairman, and the District Magistrate, the Chairman of the District Council and Prof. Gangumei Kabui as members to examine the problem of education of customary laws of the different tribes of the district. A problem arose in the matter of interpretation of the nature of chiefship among the Anals. One faction led by an Anal Minister of Manipur state claimed that Anal Chiefs were elected by the people; he and his supporters produced a number of documents in support of their position. An opposite faction led by a former president of parallel Naga Federal Government (Regional) contended that Anal chiefship was hereditary. This faction also produced a large number of documents in support of their contention. It later transpired that both the factions had the same objectives but had different strategies. Both were anxious to retain Anal control over the lands and forests in the territories inhabited by them. The Anal Minister felt that if the chiefship was considered as hereditary, the Government officials could bribe the Chiefs and take over the resources on behalf of the state; the faction close to the parallel government felt that the people's mobilisation was strong enough to keep the Chiefs under check and the Government would not be in a position to take over the resources because in that case huge compensation would have to be paid to the Chiefs.

The committee reported that the Chiefs during their lifetime selected their successors but such selection was subject to the confirmation by the concerned peoples.

Subsequent developments proved that both the factions were partially right and partially wrong in their assessment of the future. The Manipur Land and Land Reforms Act does not recognise community as a legal entity. On the other hand almost entire lands in the hills of Manipur are under communal occupation. Manipur state legislature decided to extend the operation of the Act to the hills. The Government would recognise only homestead lands and lands under settled agriculture as being owned by individual households; the remaining land was to be recorded as state land. In some areas, the villagers had thrown out the Chiefs forty years ago; now the villagers requested the Chiefs to lay claim as owners of the lands. The Chiefs were quick to take advantage of the development and started negotiating with the Government to pass on the land to the state if modest compensation was paid to them. A new feudalisation process was initiated through the façade of land reform and convenient interpretation of institution of self-government. However things did not take place exactly as designed by each of the parties due to intervention of different quarters including some social scientists. The details of the new development are not important to the present discourse. What has been presented here brings out the manipulative scope of the institution of self- government by picking up its elements in a selective manner.

Functional Jurisdiction of Self-governing Institutions

Functional jurisdiction of the self-governing institutions broadly extends to four categories:

A. Management of external relations;

B. Regulation of basic institutions centering family, property and various customary matters;

C. Maintenance of civic amenities;

D. Channel for introduction of 'development' activities.

In the management of external relations, particularly with the state and state functionaries, the self-governing institutions have frequently been relegated to the background. Statutory bodies of local self-government play more prominent role. But in case of confrontation with the state and state apparatus, frequently the traditional institutions do the back-seat driving or even sometimes come to the forefront. In the context of insurgency in many parts of North East India this is a matter of considerable importance.

In the regulation of basic institutions centring family, property and customary matters the traditional village headman and his associates play very important roles. Disputes are referred to them for settlement according to the prevailing norms of the concerned peoples. In case of inter village disputes some of the tribes like those belonging to Adi-group have institutional arrangement of higher order (Bane Kebang) to step in.

Petty crimes and torts are more frequently decided by statutory institutions of local self-government, as the dissatisfied party can lodge appeal to the Government court.

In the matter of maintenance of civic amenities the roles of traditional institutions and statutory bodies vary from tribe to tribe. Many tribes of Mizo-Kuki Chin group, Naga constellation and Adi constellation for instance, have age-group system, though bachelors' dormitories and spinsters' dormitories have ceased to exist in most cases. Generally these age-groups with their own functionaries operate in an autonomous manner; but they are expected to accept guidance of the traditional head of the self-government institution. The youth of the village - males and females collectively undertake such activities as clearing the access road to the village, the sources of drinking water, maintenance of supply reserve forest and tree-ring to protect the residential area from the burning shoots floating down from shifting cultivation fields.

As channels for development activities (however defined) the traditional institutions of self-government hardly play any role. The statutory bodies are more in the picture, as the requisite inputs are generally made available through such bodies.

In Nagaland an attempt has been made to synthesise the traditional structure and the new impulses. The statues in Nagaland recognise the traditional institutions of self-government. For each village, these bodies are authorised to set up a Village Development Board, which operates model schemes provided by the Government or approved by the Government; but which has also formally receive concurrence of the traditional set up. This experiment has passed through many vicissitudes. But to understand the extent of the effective or ineffective function of the V.D.Bs, the totality of the socio-political field in Nagaland must be analytically kept in view.

Operational Procedures

Operational procedures are to be considered in three aspects, *viz*, spatial aspect, participation aspect and proclamatory aspect.

Spatial aspect

Where bachelors' dormitories exist generally the village council meets there and discusses the disputed issues in the presence of all the villagers. Some sections of the Mishings are reported to meet in the village namghar (Vaisnavite community sacred house for prayer, religious discourse and ancillary activities with an aura of solemnity).

Where separate community places, having the aura of tradition in one form or the other, does not exist, the village council meets at the place of the headman or the Chief.

If the facts are disputed, the system of divination or trial by subjecting the concerned persons to ordeals in various forms is taken recourse to. Two decades ago, one student of sociology explained in a public lecture at Delhi that these procedures, particularly subjecting a person to harsh ordeal, are taken recourse to only after other methods including oath taking fails. Besides, trial by ordeal generally requires consensus of the entire community. Hence the formal procedure is of secondary importance. What is more important is the agreement among the villagers about the morality of the particular action under the given circumstances.

Once the facts are established, the behaviours of all concerned in the dispute are discussed in terms of the logic of the system and requirement of the situation. Unlike in formal law the dispute settlement in the traditional system tends to be an act of retribution rather than act of reprisal. Individual circumstances of the guilty person or persons are taken into consideration so that they can be retrieved to the community. Retaliation is not generally the objective, at the community level. But until recently before the community was involved, blood feud and retaliation at the individual or family or lineage level were practised among tribes like the Nishis of Arunachal.

At the Council meetings women were not active participants in the decision making process, almost anywhere. Even among the matrilineal societies like the Garo, the Khasi or the Jaintia, matriarchy did not have any place in public affairs. Orientation of all these peoples was patriarchal. Even then, on some occasions outstanding women personalities played important role in the traditional set up. Mention may be made of Rani Baitangi of the Mizos who faced the British officials on behalf of her people in the sixties of the 19th century.

During the Council meeting drinks were to be supplied by the aggrieved party asking for the meeting. Among many tribes drinks were provided by both the parties. After getting the facts established and hearing all concerned, the Chief pronounced the decision.

The punishment in most cases was in the form of compensatory payment to the aggrieved party and also fine to be paid to the Chief or headman who generally shared the same with the other office bearers and elders.

Challenges and Response

One of the major challenges faced by the institutions of traditional self-government is the introduction of statutory institutions of local self-government, some of which are found to be inauthentic on closer look. Arunachal Statutory Panchayats which were in existence during 1967 to April 1994 can hardly be called institutions of self-government. Density of population in Arunachal is about 10 per sq km. Here, distance from one village to another is frequently quite long. In this context Gram Panchayats were established for every 300 population, which would make face to face interaction among the concerned peoples impossible for months. On the other hand existence of the statutory Gram Panchayats tended to make traditional institutions of self-government irrelevant in the eyes of the various implementing agencies. The Gram Panchayats were however not vested with any effective power. These were operative agencies of the Anchal Samities. The Subdivisional Officer or an officer of equivalent rank was the Chairman of the Anchal Panchayat. Besides an unspecified number of officials were ex-officio members of the Anchal Panchayats. It would be a travesty of reality to call such a bureaucracy dominated body an institution of local self-government. And yet this body was vested with wide ranging powers including management and control of open sites, waste, vacant and grazing lands, not being private property and river bed. Given the facts that (a) in Arunachal bulk of the land is communal land, and not private land (b) the concept of waste and vacant land is an ambiguous one and the prevailing concept in legal epistemology is considered to be a colonial legacy, vesting such power with the panchayat samity was virtually an act of by-passing Nehru's commitment that tribal rights in respect of land would be respected. The Zilla Parishad under North East Frontier Agency Panchayat Raj Regulation 1967 had only advisory power. The challenges faced by traditional institutions of local government are really serious and there are indications that in some areas the people have not passively submitted to the challenge.

Challenge in another form is being faced in some other parts of the country. In the 1970's Awangkhul in West Manipur district was connected by motorable road with Imphal in Manipur and Silchar in Cachar. In this village slash and burn cultivation is extensively practised, the shifting cultivation cycle being about 10 years. Normally if a person does slash and burn cultivation on a plot he has the first prerogative to come back to the same land. During the intervening years he looks after the land and has the prerogative to enjoy the naturally grown produce on the land, including extraction of bamboo and timber. He has also the right to sell bamboo from this land to the co-villagers for their consumption. With the motorable road coming up, some of the villagers sold bamboo to outside contractors who removed the same by trucks. A joint meeting of the traditional village council and the village authority set up under Hill Village Authority Act 1956, decided that the individual's traditional prerogative over the land was for traditional use of the product, but sale of bamboo to outsiders for profit was a non-traditional use and the individual had no right in this matter.

The joint meeting decided that in future in case of such extraction, the royalty would go to the common village fund and would be used for running a village school. But such decision could not be uniformly adopted in all the hill villages or even in all the Rongmei Naga villages of Manipur. In this matter intervention of the state officials was sometimes found to be a negative factor. Awangkhul with history of resistance to bureaucratic intervention but at the same time of going for collective endeavour to improve the conditions of life of the village, could size up to the challenge or even counter the negative intervention of a section of officials. But the villages without such history became the victims of counter-history, that is, forces disharmonic to the ethos of the historical experiences of an entity.

Ancillary Matters

This rapid over-view brings out the fact, not very sharply perhaps, that traditional self-government is not a matter of mere structural arrangement. Structural arrangement is important, but linking up its functioning mode with the conditioning facts of history reflected in the ethos and eidos quietly (and sometimes not so quietly) prompting the peoples to action in various forms is equally important. This requires re-thinking of many assumptions and ideas that inform the policy makers and implementing agencies.

2

Traditional Self-Governing Institutions Among The Hill Tribal Population Groups in Tripura

– *J.B. Ganguly*

Introduction

The state formation process took shape in Tripura in the beginning of the 15th century when the king belonging to the Tripura tribe succeeded in establishing his authority of effective political control over the different tribal peoples living in the territory of Hill Tripura. At that time the dwellers in the hills of Tripura belonged to the following tribes :

1. The Tripura;
2. The Jamatia;
3. The Riang;
4. The Halams divided into twelve sub-tribes; and
5. The Kukis divided into two major groups, namely, the Darlong and the Lushai (Mizo).

The Bodo-speaking Tripura tribes, namely, the Tripura and the Jamatia, belonging to the Indo-Mongoloid stock migrated into Tripura in the remote past. They came here through Assam, Sylhet and Cachar in successive waves (Chatterjee, pp. 172-73). The early home of the Riangs was 'Mayanithlung' area of the Lushai (Mizo) Hills. Therefrom on account of inter-clan feuds, at one stage, a large number of Riang led by Tuikluha, Lungsika, Paisika and Tribruha moved into the kingdom of Tripura. These immigrant Riangs settled down mainly in the southern part of the kingdom (Somendrachandra Deb Barma, pp. 87-90).

The Kukis live in the Jampui Hills in the north-eastern part of Tripura and in Lushai (Mizo) Hills. The immigration of the Kukis into Tripura took place long back and as many of them continued to live in the Mizo Hills adjoining to Tripura, there had been periodic movements of these people from their habitats into the hills falling within Tripura in search of forest lands for practising slash and burn cultivation.

Somendrachandra Deb Barma maintains that the Halams are a branch of the Kuki tribe. These Kukis who initially accepted the suzerainty of the Tripura king came to be known as the Halams. They were originally the inhabitants of 'Khurpuitabhum', which is a hilly area lying in the north of Manipur (ibid., p. 80).

The two Buddhist tribes, named the Chakma and the Mag, migrated into Tripura much later. The Garos and the Khasis came from Assam during the early decades of the last century. They were followed by the Munda, Oraon, Santhal, Bhil, Bhutia, Lepcha, etc. who came as tea garden labourers from Bihar, Orissa and Madhya Pradesh and also re-migrated from Assam.

There are at present all-told nineteen scheduled tribes in Tripura. But only the Tripura, Riang, Jamatia, Halam and Kuki (including the Lushai) may be taken as the early indigenous tribal population groups in Tripura. Therefore in this paper an account of the traditional self-governing institutions of these tribal peoples is given.

Origin of Tribe and Polity

The earliest form of social formation of the humans is the tribe. As Jawaharlal Nehru wrote : "..... the first advance in civilization that early man made was to combine together in packs, or as these are called, tribes. They began to work together. There was what is called cooperation. Each man had to think of the tribe first and then about himself..... (1945, p. 37).

As the tribes learnt about agriculture they began to settle down in villages. These villages became the territorial units of identity for the respective groups of families belonging to the same tribe living therein. Economic, cultural and religious activities came to be organized village-wise. When a group of men live together there is bound to arise inter-personal and inter-family feuds. Since villages were autonomous, inter-village disputes had to be settled either by negotiation or force, that is, inter-village war. And inter-village disputes could arise over enjoyment of access to forests, land, water etc resources. Plundering of village by neighbouring villages for looting food and other consumables and even humans for using as slaves was also frequent. Both for organizing such raids as also for defending the village against such onslaughts the villagers required to be organized and led by someone. This leader could also settle interpersonal and inter-family disputes. In Nehru's word again : "Now if people work together they must act in an orderly way. If everyone were to do just what he pleased there would not be much of the tribe left. So someone has to become the leader .... The tribes of men also choose the strongest man amongst them as their leader. As there was a great deal of fighting to be done the strongest man was chosen (ibid., p.37)".

This has been the genesis of the emergence of tribal polity. Initially the basis for grouping together of humans was kinship or blood relationship and over time it broadened into common ethnicity. Then the tribe emerged as the basic unit of social, cultural and political formations. The spread of the tribe soon exceeded the limit of the village. That is, a tribe could spread over a number of villages. The question of selecting the leader both at the village and tribal levels arose. This is indeed a political process however elementary it may be. "Man is by nature a political animal" so said Aristotole. At the tribal stage, at first, the political activities related to the selection of the Chief. Gradually such activities were extended to the shaping and running of self-governing institutions. Such systems were not in every case consciously devised and given forms and shapes. These evolved to serve the people's needs and aspirations in the given circumstances. These were also to help the early humans survive by adopting themselves to the ecological environment.

The needs of the people were conditioned by the method and instruments of production which included hunting, gathering and, of course, farming. The maintenance of ecological balance was also a limiting factor. On these factors depended the possibility of production of surplus. As and when it became possible to produce more than the subsistence needs, the appropriation of the surplus and its accumulation assumed importance. Consequently the system of ownership of private property took shape. All these developments brought about changes in the forms and functioning of the tribal polity. Some changes also happened under the impact of endogenous impositions. For example, when a tribe was subjugated by a stronger tribe or a more powerful authority like a king and was incorporated into his kingdom, the former's self-governing system underwent changes. All the changes might not be the imposition of the external authority, some changes might be the result of the tribe's responses to the encounters with the external authority.

The historical period of the Tripura kingdom started with the reign of Mahamanikya whose original name was Chhengthung Fa. According to Ramesh Majumdar, in the early part of the 15th century Mahamanikya acquired "the extensive tract lying between Chittagong and Sylhet and established a new kingdom" (Majumdar, p.486). The state formation process in Tripura thus dates back to this period of history (for details see, Ganguly, 1985, pp. 146-159). During that period, as we have already noted above, the Tripura, Riang, Jamatia, Halam and Kuki tribes lived in Tripura kingdom. All these tribes practised shifting cultivation to produce food-grains, vegetables, cotton, sesame (oilseed), etc. They collected forest products freely for meeting their innumerable needs. They reared poultry and pigs and also collected meat by hunting wild animals. They did fishing in the rivers and rivulets. They also practised the art of weaving. The self-governing institutions of these tribes had many common features as these reflected their methods of production of food and other necessaries, the instruments of production applied and their relations with the Tripura king. Such institutions were not obviously static, they underwent changes with the development of new methods as well as modes of production associated with generation and appropriation of surplus, growth of ownership of private property, use of money in exchanging goods and services and also for storing wealth, etc.

In the absence of historical records, it is not possible to give an authentic account of the self-governing systems of these tribes as they obtained before the Tripura kingdom was established. Information about these bodies is also scanty for the early period of the rule of the Tripura Rajas. Some accounts of the tribal systems of self-administration are available with the *Rajmala,* the chronicle of the Rajas of Tripura which was compiled and edited by Kaliprasanna Sen, the *Rajmala* written by Kailas Chandra Singha which differs from the former in many respects, the Census Report by Somendrachandra Deb Barma for 1931 (1340 Tripura Era) named "*Census Bibarani*" (in Bengali), etc. Recently some social scientists and researchers have collected details about these institutions directly from the concerned leading tribal personalities and have published their findings. These are our main sources for compiling the narratives of traditional self-governing institutions of the five tribal population groups in Tripura. Though no definite period could be ascribed to the existence of these institutions, it could be presumed that these institutions functioned during the later period of the rule of the Tripura Rajas.

The tribals had their own systems of administration at the levels of the tribe as well as the village. In some cases there were regional level functionaries also. These bodies mainly dealt with the allotment of lands to individual households for jhuming, settling inter-personal or inter-household disputes, administration of the customary regulations about marriage, divorce, inheritances of movable property, etc. They also regulated religious performances, festivals and rituals. Dates for festivals and pujas were fixed by them. The self-governing authorities acted as the liaising agencies between the Raja and his nobles and officials and the tribe as well as the villagers as the case may be. For example, generally the Chiefs collected taxes from the individual households for paying to the king's court. The village authority fixed the dates for communal hunting and fishing and even organized the villagers for such cooperative ventures and distributed the collections among the villagers. Some developmental activities like the building and maintenance of paths, sources of water-supply, etc. were also looked after by this authority. What care for the orphans, old and the disabled persons in the village was to be taken was also decided by the same body. Thus it may be said that the tribal self-governing bodies performed administrative, judicial and even some developmental functions. In keeping with the egalitarian ethos simple social security measures were also taken by them.

For comprehending such roles of the self-governing authorities we have to consider the changes that were affecting the tribal mode of production. We have mentioned above that the tribal peoples during the period in question mainly practised shifting cultivation to produce their food and even some cash crops like cotton, oilseeds and vegetables. Later they also started producing another cash crop, namely, a variety of jute called *mesta* which could be grown on high lands. They got cash by selling the surplus cash crops for paying house tax to the Raja who had imposed this tax on every tribal family for practising slash and burn cultivation in the forest lands. The rates varied from tribe to tribe depending on the particular tribe's relations with the Raja. The tribal producers had also to pay tax on cotton, oilseeds and *mesta* when these items were exported out of the kingdom. The tribal households also needed cash for procuring salt, tools, utensils and many other consumer goods and even yarns for weaving cloth from the weekly markets.

The ownership of private property (mainly movable property) already prevailed. Since the later half of the nineteenth century some tribal families, encouraged by the policy of the Raja, took to settled plough cultivation on valley lands reclaimed and owned by them under the land laws of the Rajas. As a result of this some form of economic stratification based on the ownership of land and other assets including cash marked the tribal village structure. This transition may be regarded as the one from, what Samir Amin calls, 'primitive-communal' to the 'tribute-paying' mode of production (Amin, 13-14). The forms and structure of self-governing institutions of the tribal peoples and the powers exercised and functions discharged by them had direct relations with such emerging socio-economic formations.

We may now turn to give brief accounts of the self-governing institutions of the different tribes. First, the village administrative system of the Tripuras who constitute the largest tribe in terms of population.

The Tripura

Since the Rajas of Tripura belonged to this tribe there was

no centralized self-governing authority covering the whole tribe other than the king and his court where some of their traditional customary rituals and functions were continued to be performed. The Tripuras who were directly related to the Raja, either by blood or by marriage were known as the '*thakur*'. They were the king's nobles and were very close to the ruler. They assisted him in matters of administration by holding offices under the king as also by liaising between the king and the subordinate chieftains of other tribes. The Tripuras other than the 'thakur' were divided into twelve title-holders or '*hadas*' and were assigned specific duties in the king's court and the household. Somendrachandra Deb Barma, in his Census Report for 1931 (1340 T.E.) has given details of the specific functions performed by the persons belonging to the twelve '*hadas*' (pp. 61-64). "It is possible that this stratification within the Tripura tribe", maintains Bani Prasanna Misra, "was a degenerated version of self-governing institution prevailing among them in earlier periods" (p. 46).

Debapriya Debbarma, a Tripuri scholar, has given the following outline of their traditional village self-governing system (pp. 62-64).

In each village every year, just before the *jhuming* (shifting cultivation) starts, the adult male members assemble and through free and frank discussion select one among them as their Chief or '*sardar*', who is also called the '*Chaudhuri*', and other members of the village council. They hold office ordinarily for a period of one year. The *Chaudhuri* is assisted in his work by the '*karbari*' who functions something like the secretary to the Chief. Another office-bearer designated as the '*khandal*' does the work of circulating the decisions of the Council or of the Chief among the fellow villagers. The Council meets in the house of the Chief. In fact the *Chaudhuri's* house is used as the office of the council.

Women are totally excluded from the membership of the Council. They cannot also attend or take part in the deliberations of the Council excepting for the occasion when any woman is summoned by the Council to defend herself against any charge framed against her or to give witness in any case being tried by the Council. Thus the women are excluded from the decision making process in the self-governing system.

The number of members of the council is not fixed, it may vary from time to time according to the exigency of the circumstances. Though the normal term of membership and chiefship is one year, it may be extended beyond that period if the villagers feel that the Chief and the members of the Council have been doing their work satisfactorily. Similarly the term can even be shortened if the villagers are dissatisfied with the functioning of the Council. But such instances are extremely rare.

The main functions of the Council are to ensure that the individual families take up forest lands for shifting cultivation in accordance with their customary practices and to fix the dates and places of worship of different deities some of which are associated with the starting of jhuming by cutting forests, burning the dry debris, sowing of seeds, harvesting of crops, etc. The Chief collected the house tax payable by each jhumia family of his village for handing over to the king's officials. Every year on the *Vijaya Dashami* day the king invited the tribal Chiefs to the capital, Agartala, where a grand dinner was held for them. The Chiefs came to the capital with the collected taxes both in cash and kind and handed over to the king's officers along with other tributes. This was known as "*hashom bhojan*". By attending this feast the Chiefs belonging to the different tribes confirmed their loyalty to the Raja.

An important function of the Council is to settle disputes among the families on any issue. The disputes are mainly related to the use of land by the individual households, marriage relations, etc. Moreover it also tries all cases that are brought before it. For trying such cases the parties to the disputes are asked to report to the Council's meeting and are given full opportunity for speaking out their respective positions. After the hearing is over the Council members come to a consensus about the punishment to be given. The Council also deals with personal feuds within the family.

Ordinarily, after the guilt is established, the offender or offenders are made to pay a fine in cash or kind. The fine is often collected in the form of a few bottles of rice-beer which is shared by the Council members and the villagers present on the spot. The erring family may even be required to arrange for a feast for the villagers as a whole. On rare occasions "the Council would go to the extent of flogging the offenders for a serious offence or defying the (customary) rule" (Debbarma, 1983, p 63). An idea about the Tripura's traditional concept of crime and punishment can be formed from the following instance of deciding a case by the Council:

> "When a girl became pregnant before her marriage the case was forwarded to the Council. The Council identified the boy and arranged their ceremonial marriage. In similar cases if the boy and girl bore any blood relation the boy and the girl were convicted and excommunicated. In such case, the boy and the girl would come back to the village if they agreed to offer a feast to the villagers. Then their marriage would become legal and the couple got social acceptance." (ibid.)

The Riang

The second largest tribe, the Riangs, are a well-knit ethnic group having a rigid, well-ordained and well-structured self-governing system. Details about this system are obtainable from the "Census Bibarani" for 1931 (1340 T.E.) compiled by Somendrachandra Debbarma, Census Officer of Tripura. Recently Jagadish Ganchaudhuri has collected information about the Riangs and published that in his book, "The Riangs of Tripura". In that book also particulars about the Riang's self-governing system have been given.

The Ray or *Kami Kachhkao* is the supreme head or king of the Riang tribe as a whole. Under him are the following functionaries:

Chapia Khan : The next Ray in line. In the absence of the existing Ray he becomes the new Ray. Of course he assists and advises the *Kami Kachhkao* in administering the affairs of the tribe. Ganchaudhuri has designated him as the 'Prime Minister'.

Chapia : He is future *Chapia Khan*. Ganchaudhuri has treated this post as equivalent to that of a minister.

Chheng Krak : The Chief of the army.

Since the Riangs were spread over different parts of Tripura their habitats were divided into three zones marked by the three rivers, namely, the Muhuri in the south, the Gomati in the middle and the Khowai in the north-east parts of Tripura. The Ray appointed three Chiefs for the three zones. These Chiefs are known as *Huklai Chaudhury* whose main duties are to organize the annual puja *Hamui taimi,* to maintain inter-village communication and to serve as the link between the Ray and the village Chiefs.

After the whole of Tripura came under the rule of the Tripura Raja, the position of the Riang Ray and his subordinate functionaries at the all Tripura and zonal levels became less effective as rulers and administrators. But they have continued to wield much influence in social, religious and cultural affairs of the Riangs. The Ray has a tremendous moral influence over the Riangs and he is reverentially treated as the symbol of Riang solidarity. This is maintained by the practice of community worships of the Riangs performed at the source of the Gomati. Referring to this practice in the twenties Debbarma writes (translated from Bengali):

"... the whole community of the Riangs assemble every year for jointly worshipping the rivers Gomati, Karnafuli, Muhuri, Feni and performing *Ker Puja, Chitragupta Puja, Matangi Puja, Tripura Sundari* and *Lakshmi Puja,* etc. or any one or more of such pujas with great festivities. For such community worships ten to twelve hundred rupees are spent every year. This money comes from the collections of subscriptions. Each Riang family contributes to the fund. By organizing such community worships they show their ethnic unity. It is only after all of them assemble at the site of the puja that the actual work of puja is started. The responsibility of organizing the puja rests with the *Katar defa* (clan) ...."

"Their community worship is marked by a special significance. On the occasion of the puja the leading Riang Chiefs hold a meeting. At this meeting settlement of all kinds of disputes among the Riangs and trials of crimes take place. If at the trial anybody is fined, the fine money is collected at once and is deposited into the tribe's common fund. If there is any saving out of the puja subscriptions after meeting all expenses on account of the puja that amount is also credited into the common tribal fund. A part of this fund goes to the members of the *Katar defa* and the balance is spent on the welfare of the community".

"Such community worships of the Riangs serve the purpose of political, religious and social objectives. In such assemblies of the whole Riang tribe the individual members of the tribe can meet each other, exchange their views on different issues and express their tribal solidarity and loyalty to their Chiefs. Such meetings help to enhance tribal and social welfare. This opens up the possibility of strengthening the vitality of the tribe." (p. 75)

At the village level the Riang village council is headed by the Chief called *kamifang*. The other office-bearers are the *karpang* (store-keeper), *akchai* (priest), *kandal* (peon-cum-bodyguard) and *daoa* (messenger). The adult male villagers select their Chief and other office-bearers of the council through discussion and arriving at a consensus. They hold office normally for a period of one year coinciding with the period of the jhum cycle. Women are not allowed to participate in the deliberations in the council or in selecting the office-bearers. "If the office-bearers were found faithful", writes Gan Chaudhuri, "their term of office would be renewed. Besides efficiency, supernatural blessing was believed to be an important factor. If a Chief was liked by the gods, no clash, quarrel, crop failure, disease, distress, draught, etc. could occur, otherwise all these misfortunes would follow. In that case another person would be selected." (p. 79)

The Chief's house is the meeting place of the council. Also almost every evening the elderly male villagers assemble in his house for gossiping over a smoke and deliberating on different issues. Since much of the Chief's time is spent on dealing with the affairs of the villagers, he has very little time at his disposal for minding his own farming activities. In such matters, therefore, he gets the free services of the villagers. The Chief also acts as the representative of the villagers before the king's officers when they visit the village on official business.

"The main functions of the village council were", notes Gan Chaudhuri, "the settlement of disputes, trial of cases, distribution of hill slopes for shifting cultivation, organisation of communal ceremonies and festivals for the peace and prosperity of the settlement, looking after the defence of the village, helping the poor and the sick of the village, collection of government tax and assisting the government officials on tour."

The council tries cases by applying the principle of natural justice as there are no formal codes of law. The accused is given full freedom of defence. Though normally the Riangs are not given to giving false witness there may be cases of furnishing false evidence and denying the charge stubbornly. In such cases decisions were taken ultimately by subjecting the alleged offender to undergo certain traditional ordeals as is the practice among some other tribes.

The Jamatia

The Jamatiyas, the third largest tribe in Tripura, have the most elaborately structured three-tier traditional self-governing institutions with well-defined functions. Though they are mostly concentrated in Udaipur and Amarpur subdivisions, some of them also live in the Sadar and Khowai subdivisions. Ethnically they are very close to the Tripuras. As disciplined fighting personnel they constituted the core of the Raja's armed forces. And the name, 'Jamatiya', seems to have been derived from the word 'jamat' which means a congregation of persons. The Raja's army manned by them was called *'jamat'*. Since their main occupation was to fight for the king the whole community was known as the Jamatiya. Their spoke language is *kogbarak*, that is, the same as that of the Tripuras. Only their intonation is slightly different.

Since they worked in the Raja's army they were exempted from the payment of house tax. They also enjoyed certain other privileges. Among the tribes of Tripura the general conditions of this group of people was much better. Because, as Somendrachandra Debbarma has mentioned (*op. cit.*, p. 69), most of the Jamatiya families had taken to settled plough cultivation leaving the practice of shifting cultivation behind. They had become attached to the system of ownership of land and they had settled villages instead of shifting villages. As a result they had been prospering with the growing flow of income and acquiring of assets through saving of income.

This marked difference from other tribes is also reflected in their well-organized and well-run representative from of self-governing institutions. Prodip Nath Bhattacharjee has recorded in detail particular about these institutions and their functions in his book, The *Jamatiyas of Tripura* (1983). Largely based on his findings (pp. 40-44) the three-tier self-governing institutions of the Jamatiyas are indicated below.

At the village level there is the council called *luku* which is headed by *chokdiri* (the Chief), who is elected by the senior male members of the village. To be elected as a *chokdiri* one must be a married person having wife and children. He must also be economically a resourceful person. *Chokdiri* is assisted in his work by two or more *khandals* probably elected in the same manner as the *chokdiri*.

At the regional level, which covers thirty to fifty *lukus* contiguous to each other, there is the regional council known as *moyol*. At the head of *moyol* there are two *moyol panchay* who are elected by all the *adongs* of the *lukus* falling within the *moyol*. The *chokdiri* of every *luku* appoints two *adongs* who represent the *luku* at the annual conference of the supreme council (*hoda*). The *moyol panchays* must be also economically resourceful family men.

For the whole Jamatiya community there is the supreme council termed as *hoda*. The supreme Chief of the Jamatiya is called *hoda-okra* who is elected by all the *adongs* of all the *lukus* of the Jamatiya community. Initially there was only one *hoda-okra* but later they came to have two *hoda-okras* - one for Udaipur and one for Amarpur Divisions. They are elected by the *adongs* of all the *lukus* at the annual conference held in the month of *Agrahayana* (November - December), that is, after the harvesting season is over. Normally they hold office for a period of five years. The eligibility for becoming an *okra* is that one "must be religious minded wellknown personality with adequate experience of the functions of their traditional administrative organisations and customary laws" (*op. cit.*, p. 41). As for the lower level Chief, he also must be a good resourceful family man having wife and children.

The *lukus* settle minor disputes occurring in the village. For trying cases the *chokdiri* seeks the help of senior villagers who constitute something like a jury. It is an important duty of the *chokdiri* to maintain contacts with *moyol panchay* and the *hoda-okra*. Along with the *adong* he also takes part in the annual meeting of the supreme council. "He supervises all sorts of social functions like marriage, death or any other rituals and also looks after the welfare of the village"(ibid.).

The Chief function of the *moyol panchays* is to settle inter-village disputes in consultation with the *chokdiris*. *Moyol panchays* may refer the case to *hoda-okra* for final settlement.

"The *hoda-okra* is the formal spokesman of the entire Jamatiya community. His verdict is final. The function of the *hoda* is to arrange some festivals like *Goriya Puja, Balangswamani, Ganga Puja* etc. for the welfare of the entire Jamatiya community. Besides the religious function the *hoda* has judicial functions too. All kinds of cases like divorce, adultery, kidnapping, anti-social activities and complicated cases which could not be solved by the village council and regional council are dealt with by the *okra*. The *hoda* is the highest court of appeal vested with highest degree of legislative, administrative and judicial powers" (ibid.).

As a later development of the system of self-governing institutions, the Jamatiya brought into being the advisory council or *Upadesta Committee* consisting of eight executive members. The main objective of the creation of this body has been to make it possible for the young and educated Jamatiyas to be associated with the running of the affairs of the community. It is expected that they will be able to bring in the modern and scientific outlook in guiding the activities of the councils. Bhattacharjee also maintains that this advisory council 'acts as a check on the dictatorial tendencies of the *okras*'.

The *modus operandi* of the judicial process as recorded by Bhattacharjee is worth noting. Any member of the community can lodge a complaint against any other member to the *chokdiri* of his *luku* on payment in kind of a bottle or rice beer or in cash amounting to rupee one. On the date fixed for the hearing at the *chokdiri's* house both the parties report with their respective witnesses. At first the accuser speaks explaining the charge. Then the defendant is given the chance to defend himself. After that the witnesses on the both the sides make their submissions. Then the whole matter is referred to the jury consisting of the old and influential members of the village for a decision. Of course the *chokdiri* passes the judgement in consultation with the jury. As a punishment for ordinary crimes a fine is imposed on the guilty to be paid in cash or kind. In serious cases of violation of community's traditional values the offender may even be ostracised from the village and the community.

"When the *chokdiri* fails to settle any case or his judgement is not accepted by either of the parties, the case is referred to the *moyol panchay* who in turn sends it to a non-related village council for settlement. But the *panchay's* judgement is not final even here and one can appeal against his judgement to the supreme council. The *okras* do not call a meeting in their houses but select any village council as a place for hearing of the case. In this matter the *moyol panchay* and the *chokdiri* in whose jurisdiction the case originally belonged must be present during the trial of the case" (*op. cit.*, 42).

From the above account it is clear that the Jamatiya judicial process is very elaborate having the scope for filing appeals to the successive higher self-governing authorities. The hierarchy of the administrative and judicial bodies is very clearly defined.

The Kuki and the Lushai

Among the Kukis there was the Chief or the Raja, called *Halamcha* who led his community in its relations with other communities and tribes and also decided about the extension of village settlements to new areas. He was the ultimate interpreter of customs and conventions of the tribe. At the village level, the Chief called *Sangalthong* was elected by the villagers from among a certain group of families. The person so elected could not decline to hold the office. If he did so, he had to pay a fine. *Sangalthong* headed the village council which included other elders. This council settled all village disputes. The grand Chief or *'Lal'* appointed some Chiefs under him for settling inter-village disputes. (Singh, p. 40). The *Halamcha* collected taxes from the villagers and remitted to the king's court.

In his paper, 'Local Self-government in Tripura under the Manikyas' presented at a seminar on local self government in Tripura, Pratap Chaudhury has stated that all the subtribes of the Kukis had the same system of self governance. "All matters of internal village government are decided by the Chief assisted by his Council of elders or *Upas*. Although all power is theoretically in the hands of the Chief, practically speaking he will never try a case without consulting his *Upas* and as a rule three or four *Upas* try cases with the Chief. These *Upas* are appointed by the Chief and can be dismissed by him. The Chief and the *Upas* get some privilege for their social work. In dealing with the cases the Chief and the *Upas* are guided by the customary laws of the tribe concerned. A Chief who disregards the customary law is abandoned by his people" (p. 13).

Among the Kuki community one of the functions of the village Chief was to maintain properly the village water supply source. If necessary, it was to be cleaned and fenced effectively. The village paths were also kept usable by the Chief. For all such works he could engage the villagers as and when necessary.

The *Lushais* are the most advanced among the *kukichin* tribes in Tripura. They are concentrated in the Lushai and Shakan hill ranges in the northern part of the state. The village council is the most effective self-governing organization of the Lushais which regulates their economic and social activities. They have the system of election of the members of the council which consists of five to ten members depending on the size of the village. All the members of the village assemble together to elect their representatives to the village council by recording their choice on slips of paper. The members have normal term of office running into three years. The President and the Secretary of the village council are the main office-bearers who exercise a lot of administrative and economic powers in regulating the life and productive activities of the villagers. Regarding the allotment of jhum fields the President has the privilege of selecting the jhum field for his use first. For the rest the system is as follows: All the families of the village are divided into a few groups and the available jhum sites are also divided into some blocks. Thereafter the plots are allotted by drawing of lots. In the use of jhum fields due care is taken about conservation of soil. In other words, the lands are allotted for jhuming only when these are ready for jhuming again so that by premature operation of jhuming the regenerative capacity of soil is not disturbed. This is one of the unique systems of rational land use for jhuming in the hill slopes maintaining the soil conservation objectives.

The village council settles all disputes occurring in the village in accordance with the traditional codes of conduct. It also serves as the spokespersons for the villagers in dealing with the government agencies and outsiders.

The President of the village council, as mentioned by Pratap Choudhury, is entitled to have the free labour of the villagers for the construction of his house. He can also mobilize free village labour for the construction of schools, church and other commonly used public works.

The supreme authority of the Lushais is the '*Lal*' or king who was recognised by the Tripura King as such. All the presidents of the village councils were obliged to carry out the orders of the '*Lal*', who is respected by all the members of the community.

The Koloi

Although the Tripura Rajas grouped all the tribes supposedly belonging to *Kuki* group as '*Halam*' which included the so-called twelve sub-tribes, recent researches have proved that this classification was wrong. Some of the so-called sub-tribes (their number varied from twelve to eighteen) were actually exclusively separate ethnic entities. The *Kolois* are one such. Based on Pradipnath Bhattacharjee's work on the *Kolois* we are giving below an account of the traditional self-governing institutions of the *Kolois*.

The *Kolois* have well-organized self administrative system both at the village and tribe levels. Their community system of administration and judicial process are divided into a hierarchy of seven functionaries arranged from the top to bottom as given below:

Rai
↓
Galim
↓
Kanchan
↓
Gabur
↓
Jaksung
↓
Khuksung
↓
Senga

The *Rai* is the supreme Chief of the *Kolois*. To be eligible to become a *Rai* one must have acquired the experiences of serving as all the other six levels of leaders one by one. It is also ensured that one who starts as a *Senga* should get an opportunity of serving as *Khuksung, Jeksung, Gabur,* and so on. Each holder of these positions has a term of three years and by convention each of them resigns his position after three years and each one gets an opportunity to go up the hierarchy to hold the next higher position. After every three years on the *Purnima* (full moon) day of the month of *Agrahayana* (November–December) the executive committee of the community meets to elect the new *Rai*.

Though the *Rai* is the supreme authority in their society, he cannot be an autocrat as there is the provision of counteracting such tendencies, if any, are noticed. The community at large has even the powers to fine a *Rai* for any misdeed. Their system is against the growth of absolutism. No wonder, the *Rai* is normally universally respected by the

Kolois and his orders are carried out without any reservation. Therefore they are able to solve their internal problems and disputes by themselves without the intervention of any outside authority. Hardly any *Koloi* goes to the government's law courts for settling any dispute.

For every *Koloi* village there is one Chief called *choudhuri* and two *khandals* (messengers) who look after the welfare of the villagers. Of course, if there is any of the seven all-community level functionary living in a village then there will be no separate *choudhuri* for that village. The same official will do the work of the *choudhuri*.

At the lowest rung of *Koloi* hierarchy is the *Senga* and above him is the *khuksung*. Their duties are to look after the requirements of the other authorities on the occasions of trial of cases and performance of community worship and festivals. Under orders of their superior authorities they collect subscriptions from the members and carry out other duties including maintenance of peace in the society.

After only serving as a *Senga* and then as a *Khuksung* one can be a *Jaksung* who oversees the work of the formers. Similarly after holding this position for three years the *Jaksung* becomes the *Gabur* who in his turn similarly after three years' of office rises up to be a *Kanchan* and subsequently after every three years assumes the title of *Galim* and finally that of *Rai*. On all these occasions of assuming the higher title the functionary has to arrange for community feasts. Participation in such feasts is obligatory and violation of certain rules about the manner of taking part in the feasts is punishable by a fine. This system ensures that none can become a *Rai* who has not been associated with the *Koloi* self-governing process for a period of at least twenty years.

The *Kolois* have also a separate executive authority for drawing up and execution of developmental programmes for the community. There are four executive functionaries of this body, namely, *Kaithar, Barising, Mudi* and *Muila* arranged in order of the hierarchy from the bottom upwards. In this case also the term of office for each post is three years and one has to serve for three years at the position below the one which one will assume. They are associated with the organization of community worships besides looking after development activities. (Bhattacharjee, 1980, pp. 27-35).

Concluding Remark

The above brief sketches of the traditional self-governing institutions of the major tribal population groups of Tripura are not exhaustive and complete pictures of the systems concerned. These are based on some recent studies on the tribes in question. The authors of these studies have largely depended on heresay and oral testimony of some members of the tribes under study. In such cases objectivity cannot be always maintained. It would, however, be reasonable to assert that traditionally each tribe was ruled by its Chief whose office was not, normally, hereditary. The village council was the basic unit to dispense with justice and mobilize the villagers for collective action both for productive (including hunting and gathering) and defensive (also aggressive) purposes. Tribal villages, by and large, were autonomous entities for all such activities.

However, the tribe was indeed a supra-village authority which looked after the common tribal interests and maintained tribal solidarity. For ensuring this there was a hierarchy of leaders at the tribal, regional and village levels. The leader of the whole tribe was the most powerful among the functionaries and he was assisted by a number of office-bearers. The office of the store-keeper seems to be common among the tribes. This is indication of the fact that some collections, obviously in kind, were made from the individual families for meeting the needs of the officials as well as those who were in distress.

These tribal self-governing systems stand out as the ones which strictly excluded the participation of women in their workings. It is indeed a paradox that even as women participate in productive activities of the society very intensely they had no place in the decision-making process in the society. This is a serious weakness of the traditional tribal self-governing system. This denial of opportunity to the women to take part in the decision-making process at the village and community levels has been responsible for the appearance of many a non-traditional social evils in the tribal villages in Tripura in the recent times. For example, whereas traditionally the tribal groom had to work in his would be father-in-law's house for a period of two to three years or to pay in kind or cash in lieu of rendering that free labour to be eligible to marry the bride, now-a-days, the bride's parents are required to pay dowry to the groom's parents at the time of the marriage.

Secondly, all over the hill villages destruction of forests for commercial purposes, that is, other than for shifting cultivation, has been severely affecting the welfare of the tribal people. For such denudation of forests has been causing drying up of the sources of water supply as also of minor forest products so badly needed by the villagers. The traditional tribal male village leadership has not only failed to stop the process but in many cases have been active partners with others in bringing about such a catastrophe. But the tribal women show better appreciation of the need for conservation of forests and water resources as they are more directly concerned with the collection of firewood and other minor forest products and fetching water for meeting the family's needs. The women are pragmatic, hard-working and even forward-looking. Moreover, these days tribal women are becoming literate and educated. They are also getting themselves organized by joining women's organizations concerned with social, cultural, political and economic activities. I said elsewhere, which I repeat here:

"It has been my impression that no village development plan can be prepared and implemented without the active involvement of the women of the village" (1993, p. 79).

Again, one of the factors responsible for the alienation of tribal lands in the tribal villages is that the tribal women have not been given any shares of ownership of land as acquired by the tribal families during the rule of the Tripura Raja, or later, on lands as allotted by the government under *jhumia* settlement and several other schemes. The upshot of all this is that in the new set up of village level self-governing system as also at the higher levels women must be given active roles. In this respect the new system of Panchayati Raj envisaged under the Constitution (73rd Amendment) Act. 1992 seems to be the desirable arrangement.

All over Tripura including the tribal villages Panchayati Raj was introduced in 1962 by adopting the Uttar Pradesh Panchayats Act. This meant the replacement of the traditional tribal village councils, in whatever diluted form these still existed, by the village panchayats. The members of the panchayats were elected by the villagers including women. The candidates fought elections under the banner of different political parties. Still representation of women was few and far between. The panchayats received funds from the government for village development and relief works. Of course the amounts were never adequate. But the tribal villages thus received funds from outside which was quite a new experience. In spite of this, in the social, religious and cultural spheres as also in settling disputes and trying of cases involving tribals as the accusers and the accused the role of traditional tribal Chiefs and village councils, consisting of the village elders, still continues. It is extremely rare for any tribal to take any case involving a fellow tribal to the government's court of law. All such cases are tried by the village community and the offenders are brought to book in accordance with the traditional customary laws and conventions though these are not yet codified.

Shyamacharan Tripura, former president of the *Tripura Upajati Juba Samitee,* has claimed that even cases of murders are tried by the community and if the guilt is proved death sentences are pronounced and carried out without the knowledge of the government. No tribal ever seeks government's intervention in such matters, so strong seems to be the tribal's trust in his traditional customary sense of crime and punishment. This is the position taken by Shyamacharan Tripura. A question, however, comes to mind. Is the submission of the common tribal to the *modus operandi* of the so-called community trial and punishment is due to his genuine respect for traditional values and leadership, or is it an indication of his helplessness against continued stanglehold of the traditional Chiefs who have assumed feudal characteristics of enjoying several privileges under the cover of respect for the old tribal customs and beliefs? Some of the elements of the tribal self-governing system suggest the possibility of the emergence of feudal ingredients in a subtle form in the tribal polity. For example, among the Jamatiyas, only those who are economically resourceful can become Chiefs at different levels. It is also pertinent to note that to counteract the exercise of autocratic powers by the *hoda okra* it was necessary to constitute an Advisory Council. But whether it has been effective is very doubtful. Then among some tribal communities the village Chiefs and community leaders are entitled to some special privileges like the enjoyment of priority in the selection of jhum sites and the right to have free labour of the villagers. About the Riangs, Shyamcharan Tripura himself has stated that (1993, p. 4) anyone who is wealthy and powerful can become a Chowdhury and assumes the right of trying cases. Since the fine money is appropriated by the Chowdhury himself the question of personal gain and loss influences the passing of judgement. Therefore there is dissatisfaction among the Riangs against the traditional system of trial and punishment.

Initially Tripura was not included in the list of states where Autonomous District Councils were constituted under the Sixth Schedule of the Constitution. The model of ADC was basically conceived to ensure autonomy of the tribal people (having a long tradition of having self-governing bodies which functioned democratically and settled their disputes in accordance with their own customs and beliefs) in managing their own affairs at the level of the district and to preserve the tribal identities and to protect the interests of tribals in their lands and other resources. In response to the continued demand for having an ADC under the Sixth Schedule of the Constitution, the Constitution was amended in 1984 (forty-ninth amendment) to provide for the constitution of ADC in Tripura. Earlier in 1982 Tripura Tribal Areas Autonomous District Council was formed under an Act of the State Government. Finally, in 1985 the TTAADC was constituted under the Sixth Schedule. It covers the tribal villages all over the state spread over all the three districts. Since then the tribal villages have ceased to have panchayats. There is a provision in the Sixth Schedule for the establishment of village committees or councils by the ADC. But it is only recently that the TTAADC has got a bill approved of by the State Government for the establishment of village councils. The provisions of the village council law need to be closely examined before any opinion can be voiced about its appropriateness in the existing conditions.

References

Amin, Samir (1979), *Unequal Development*, Oxford University Press.

Bhattacharjee, Prodip Nath (1980), *Lokabritter Aloke Koloi Sampraday* (in Bengali), Department of Scheduled Tribe and Scheduled Caste Welfare, Govt. of Tripura, Agartala.

Bhattacharjee, Prodip Nath (1983), *The Jamatiyas of Tripura*, Department of Scheduled Tribe and Scheduled Caste Welfare, Govt. of Tripura, Agartala.

Chatterjee, S.K. (1950), 'Kirata-Jano - Kriti', *Journal of the Asiatic Society of Bengal, Letters,* Vol. XVI, 1950, No. 2.

Choudhury, Pratap (1991), *Local Self-Government in Tripura under the Manikyas, Proceedings of the seminar on local self-government ion Tripura held at Women's College,* Agartala on 22 and 23 November 1991.

Deb Barma, Debapriya (1983), *Treatise on Traditional Social Institutions of the Tripuri Community,* Directorate of Research, Department of Welfare for Scheduled Tribes and Schedule Castes, Govt. of Tripura.

Debbarma, Somendrachandra (1941/1343 Tripura Era), *1340 Tripura Saner Tripura Rajuer Census Bibarani,* (in Bengali), Census Office, Royal Government of Tripura.

Gan Chaudhuri, Jagdis (1983), *The Riangs of Tripura,* Directorate of Research, Deptt. of Welfare for Scheduled Tribes and Schedule Castes, Govt. of Tripura.

Ganguly, J.B. (1985), *The Economic Content of the State Formation Process in Medieval Tripura,* Proceedings of the Annual Session of the North East India History Association, Shillong.

Ganguly, J.B. (1993), The Status of Tribal Women in the post-Jhuming Stage of Tribal Economy in Tripura, published in *Status of Tribal Women in Tripura,* Ed. Malabika Dasgupta, Vikas Publishing House Pvt. Ltd., Delhi.

Majumdar, R. C. (1380 B.E.), *The History of Bengal* (in Bengali), Calcutta.

Misra, Bani Prasanna (1976), *Socioeconomic Adjustments of Tribals,* People's Publishing House, New Delhi.

Nehru, Jawaharlal (1945), *Letters from a Father to his Daughter,* Oxford University Press.

Singh, R.G. (1976), *The Kukis of Tripura,* Directorate of Research, Deptt. of Welfare for ST. and SC., Govt. of Tripura.

Tripura, Shayamcharan (1993), In the Light of the New Panchayat Act Some Thoughts on the Autonomous District Council (in Bengali) *Dainik Sambad,* 23 August 1993.

3

Traditional Self-Governing Institutions in Tripura and The Constitution (73rd Amendment) Act

– *Mahadev Chakravarti*

Every tribe has its own socio-political organization, customs and tradition at the village level, although due to the dearth of records and documents a "thick curtain of mystery" hangs over the origin and antiquities of such practices. In princely Tripura, to quote the remarks of a Political Agent, "where the Raja's word is law, and where all dread his power in a manner almost slavish, it is hopeless to suppose that any institution can flourish which is based on a system of self-government" (Hunter, p. 496). Still, some sort of self-governing institutions were there in the past both in rural and urban Tripura, more particularly in the society of the tribal people.

In 1871 the Agartala Municipality was first instituted with the Political Agent as its Chairman, although during the princely days the institution existed only in name. That was the urban scenario. In the life and society of the tribal people in the hill areas, we had the village community, governed by the Headman or the Chief, and that was the leading characteristic of their social polity. Speaking about the hill people, particularly the Tripuris, the Political Agent wrote in 1873 : "The people were very simple, truthful and honest, until corrupted by the evil influences arising from closer intercourse with the inhabitants of the plains, and also by bad government, whereby they were left at the mercy of grasping subordinates. Every advantage was taken of their ignorance and credulity, till at length they perceived this themselves, and they now no longer hesitate to meet deceit with its own weapons" (Hunter, p. 488). This historical background is not simply a subject for study, but also a basis for action.

The impact of economy on the growth of customs and traditional self-governing institutions of the hill people cannot be underestimated. Everything in the past was *jhum*-oriented. The records and documents show how the feeble royal attempts to wean over the attention of the hill people from *jhum* to plough cultivate failed in the past, as being contrary to their tradition. In a word, *jhum* is not simply an economy, but also a culture which helped the growth of a lot of traditional institutions and customary practices.

True, everyone in Tripura in the past dreaded the Manikya kings and from that one may conclude that the administrative control of the kings over the hill people was complete, making no room for the growth of local self government. But at the same time, the geographical and ecological situation of princely Tripura should also be taken into account. While answering to the allegation of British Political Agent about lax administrative control of the Durbar over the hill people, Dewan Bejoy Kumar Sen, the Chief Secretary of the State, said in 1917 that Tripura "is an extensive and wild territory, full of deep forests, intersected with lofty ranges of hills, and interspersed with vast swamps. Necessarily its administration presented difficulties, and had to be carried on mainly through the agency of clan Chiefs, but it is hardly correct to say that the Durbar exercised no authority over it" (Misra, p. 39). Thus the geographical setting of tribal habitation consisting of flora, fauna, soil, river, hill, climate etc. and the economic means of livelihood should be taken into consideration before analysing the traditional self-governing institutions of the people.

The tribals of Tripura were very loyal to their village Chiefs. With the Manikya kings at the apex and the Chiefs in the lower village level and sometimes a Headman of a particular tribe, there was a Liaison Officer, known as 'Missip', usually selected from amongst the tribal people in the village, who acted as a link between the King and the village Chief. The tribals used to have a social hierarchy in which obedience to their age-old customary practices concerning all walks of life was a must. The names of the Chiefs were different in different tribal villages - e.g. *'Rai'* and *'Choudhuri'* in a Riang village, *'Galim'* in a Halam village, *'Roaja'* among the Noatia tribe, *'Dewan'* or *'Karbari'* among the Chakmas etc. The Maharaja of Tripura even recognised the Lushai Chief in the unaccessible Jampui Hills as 'Raja'. Thus the *jhum-* oriented life and society of the tribal people of Tripura in the hills was at the same Chief-oriented. The post of the Chief was sometimes hereditary and sometimes selected by the village elders and it differed from tribe to tribe. Removal of the Riang Chief in 1940 by the Maharaja of Tripura had such an adverse effect on the social fabric and the customary practices of the Riangs that it caused a commotion and ultimately the great Riang unrest in 1942-43 although some other socio-economic factors helped the situation. The leadership and authority of the new Riang Chief, as imposed from above, were defied and the community rituals were not performed by the common Riang people under the imposed Chief's supervision. That was the lesson of history.

Regarding traditional self-governing institutions among the Tripuri community, Debapriya Deb Barman (pp. 62-63) has pointed out about the Village Council consisting of the *Sardar* (i.e. the Chief), the *Karbari* (i.e. the Secretary to the Sardar), the *Khandal* (i.e. the messenger) and the members—as selected by the village elders. Women were debarred from participating in the council. This village council was usually formed on the eve *jhum* cultivation and normally its tenure was for one year only although it could be extended for any number of years. The village elders had the right to dissolve the council at any moment or expel any member thereof if his conduct was not conducive to the interest of the community. Usually the members sat together in the *Sardar's* house and the decision of the village council was final and supreme in every matter beginning from land dispute, marriage dispute, quarrel between villagers on any issue etc., to the harassment of women, breach of age-old customary norms and practices, time and place of worship and festival etc. In a word, the Village Council had to perform an all-embracing form of duties and the offenders were penalised usually with economic fine in cash or kind and in very serious cases to the extent of flogging for defying the customs. The problems regarding new marriages were usually solved with the distribution of a few bottles of rice-beer among the members of the Village Council. The *Khandal* circulated the message of the council among the villages. The main aim and objective of the Village Council was to honour and implement the customary laws and practices. As the customary laws had the sanction of the bulk of the community, the violator was punished by the council with the support of the majority people.

As tribal societies in the past were mostly homoge-nous, it is not possible to understand traditional self-govern-ing institutions without understanding customs and customary practices of the people, which varied from tribe to tribe. In Tripura, there are nineteen tribes with so many sub-tribes. Recently a Committee was appointed on codification of tribal customary laws, rites, land usages pattern etc. and K.D. Menon, the Chairman of the Committee, had submitted a preliminary report. But a detailed codification of the age-old customs, customary practices which had the sanction of law in the society of each and every tribe is yet to be made. Hence, a top priority should now be given on the proper codification of tribal customary laws and practices and development programmes may be drawn after taking into consideration the habits and temperament of the people.

The erstwhile princely Tripura has undergone some administrative changes which created a vacuum in so far as traditional village institutions are concerned. Tripura merged with the Indian Union on 15 October, 1949; became a Part 'C' State in 1950 and a Union Territory in 1956; acquired a Legislative Assembly in 1963 and became a full-fledged state of the Indian Union on 21 January, 1972. When Tripura was a Union Territory, the then Tripura Government had adopted the Uttar Pradesh Panchayati Raj Act of 1947 which helped the eclipse of the age-old self-governing institutions of the tribal people. No meaningful institution was created other than in name, but the traditional village institutions of the tribals were given good-bye. Hence, a vacuum was created in the tribal societies of Tripura. One Panchayat Raj Training Institute had been opened in the sixties for imparting training to the Panchayat Secretaries and non-official members of the Panchayat; but upto 1978 it was virtually a defunct institution.

Transition from the age-old practice of *jhuming* to the gradual, though very slow adoption of settled cultivation has brought about certain changes in the society and necessarily on the pattern of traditional self-governing institutions of the tribals of Tripura. So long, owing to their geo-physical isolation, the network of social relations of the tribal people remained confined structurally to a relatively small area as compared to that of the non-tribals; but gradually even the interiors of the hills have been exposed to the various agencies of modernity like the road and communication, education, parliamentary elections, government sponsored plans and projects etc. While analysing the dynamics of tribal leadership in Bihar, L.P. Vidyarthi has outlined how "the rural-bred, charismatic and tradition-oriented leadership which functioned for revitalising the tribals on the Hindu model received a set back at the hands of the Christian missionaries whose uplift programmes in the tribal villages brought about new norms of choosing leaders" (Vidyarthi, p.11). In Tripura, till the thirties of the present century, the Lushai Chief in the Jampui and Sakhan hills was practically "Ceasar and Pope both rolled into one"; but the spread of Christianity created new types of need and outlook which ultimately helped drawing the curtain on the system of age-old chieftainship and the emergence of new socio-economic forces and new types of leaders in Lushai society (Chakravarty, pp. 16-18). Thus the undercurrent flow of change is to be noticed in the life and society of some tribal people of Tripura which had its effect on traditional institutions.

Let us now have a look at the population profile of Tripura which underwent a dramatic change since 1951 and this demographic revolution created a stir in the tribal society, the fear - psychosis ultimately led to the search for identity, customs and tradition.

Table 1. Population of Tripura

Census Year	*Total Population*	*Tribal Population*	*Percentage of Tribal Population*
1941	513,010	256,991	50.09
1951	645,707	237,953	36.85
1961	1,142,005	360,070	31.53
1971	1,556,342	450,544	28.95
1981	2,053,058	583,920	28.44
1991	2,757,205	853,345	30.95

In Tripura, at present, there are 3 districts, 13 sub-divisions, 18 R.D. blocks/sub-blocks, 30 revenue circles, 182 tehsils and 856 revenue villages with 60.44% persons as literate (70.58% male and 49.65% female literacy). Other than the Agartala Municipality and 18 Notified Area Authorities for the towns, there are the Tripura Tribal Areas Autonomous District Council (TTAADC) and the Panchayats as units of local self government in Tripura.

Attempts would here be made to highlight the TTAADC and PR institutions in the light of the 73rd Amendment of the Constitution. The increasing urbanisation in and around Agartala and other sub-divisional towns has ultimately pushed a large number of tribals to take shelter in the interior places and land alienation became a burning problem. As everything in the rural society revolves round land, the solution of the land alienation question became the primary task of the self-governing institutions. As the tribals stand at uneven levels in relation to the non-tribals in terms of social, cultural, economic and political development, the question of distinct ethnic identity, distinct culture, customs and tradition, taboos and social systems naturally became prominent.

The Constitution (73rd Amendment) Act has ultimately constitutionalized the Panchayati Raj as the third stratum of government, i.e. below Central and State level. Although Article 40 of the Indian Constitution, which was incorporated at Mahatma Gandhi's insistence in the Chapter on Directive Principles of State Policy, declared that "the State shall take steps to organise village panchayats and endow them with such powers and authority as may be necessary to enable them to function as units of self-government"; for long four decades and a half this Directive Principle remained unacted upon in many states of the country. But like West Bengal, the Left Front government in Tripura on assuming power embarked upon a programme of rural resurgence and held the Panchayat election for the first time under secret ballot in 1978. Under the Tripura Panchayat Act, 1983, the second election under secret ballot was held in 1984. With the removal of the Left Front form power in February, 1988, the Panchayats were also superseded in June, 1988 and since then there was no Panchayat in Tripura. The Left Front came back to power in 1993 and the stage was set again to hold election in August, 1994, as per the Constitution (73rd Amendment) Act. In 1978, as it was a single-tier system, the total number of Gaon Sabha in Tripura was 689 and at that time there was no TTAADC. But as the Tripura Panchayat Act, 1993 shall extend to the areas excluding the Municipality, Notified Area and the TTADC; as a result in a three-tier system there will now be 525 Gram Panchayat, 16 Panchayat Samiti and 3 Zilla Parishad. The Tripura Panchayat Act, 1993, was enacted in conformity with the purpose, substance and direction of the Constitution (73rd Amendment) Act, 1992, to endow the Panchayat with such functions and powers so that it may become a vibrant institution of local self government at the rural level with greater participation of people in managing their own affairs besides imparting certainty, continuity and democratic content and dignity aiming, among other things, at the realisation of economic and social justice.

In 1957, the Balvantrai Mehta Committee saw the PR system as a means of involving grass-root people in an apolitical way and as a link between local leaders and the government. In 1978 the Ashok Mehta Committee recommended two-tier PR system,involving political parties not only for power to the people but for strengthening the planning process at the micro-level. In 1983 we have got C.H. Hanumanth Rao's Working Group on District Planning. In 1985 C.V.K. Rao Committee also recommended strengthening of the Zilla Parishad and district level planning, as well as close integration of block and village for lower level planning. In 1986-87 the L.M. Singhvi Committee also recommended involving the PR institutions in the planning process and like the Ashok Mehta Committee suggested some suitable constitutional amendment for the purpose. Thus all the Committees since independence had recommended in their own way the steps to be taken for strengthening of the local self government and to involve the people at the grass-roots in the planning process. But what was the actual outcome even after the recommendations of so many Committees to give power to the people?

The Constitution (64th Amendment) Bill, which was passed by the Lok Sabha in August, 1989, was defeated in the Rajya Sabha. But the Constitution (73rd Amendment) Act by according constitutional status to the PR institutions in the rural areas and the Constitution (74th Amendment) Act to the Nagar Palikas in the urban areas in the country, through near unanimous adoption by both the Houses of Parliament and ratification by most of the State Legislatures, are now being implemented. Though belated, it is a very bold step and definitely goes a long way—if implemented in letter and spirit—in enabling these grass-root self-governing units to function as truly constitutional democratic bodies and thereby fulfilling the dream of 'power to the people'.

While there are certain provisions in the Constitution (73rd Amendment) Act as mandatory, e.g. establishment of a three-tier system of PR in the States (excepting those whose population does not exceed 20 lakhs), reservation of seats and also the offices of chairpersons for the SCs and STs in proportion to their population, reservation of one-third seats including the office of chairpersons for women under various categories, an assured term of five years to all Panchayats, constitution of Finance Commission and also an Election Commission for Panchayats in each State etc., there are certain other provisions left to the discretion of the states concerned. In conformity with the above guidelines, the Tripura Panchayat Act was passed in 1993.

Table 2. Panchayats in Tripura: 1994

Gram Panchayat	*Panchayat*	*Samiti*	*Zilla Parishad*
Total Number	525	16	3
Total Seats	5427	196	70
Scheduled Caste (Reserved)	1255	48	15
Scheduled Tribe (Reserved)	696	26	7
General Seats	3476	122	48
Seats Reserved for Women	1809	67	24

In a small State like Tripura, where the total population is only about 18 lakh according to 1991 Census and where the total number of voters for the Panchayat election is only 9,76,784 in 1994, the point is raised by many academics whether such an elaborate three-tier structure for the PR was at all necessary. Again, considering the administrative expenditure involved in the creation of the Panchayat Election Commission, the task could have been entrusted to the Chief Electoral Officer of the State who has to conduct a number elections throughout the year. Again, regarding reservation of seats for SCs and STs, it may be noted that as per provisions of the Constitution the ratio of SC and ST population to the total population in a Panchayat as per the latest published Census data are on the basis of revenue villages which are different from the village Panchayats. In the past, Census data for smaller habitations known as Census villages were available; but now we have only revenue villages whose units are usually larger and different from village Panchayats. Hence, a clear population profile of the village Panchayats should be made available to determine the reservation and other issues.

Although there is the TTAADC for the predominantly tribal areas, from the total seats reserved for the STs in the PR system (696 in the Gram Panchayat, 26 in the Panchayat

Samiti and 7 in the Zilla Parishad) we may have an idea of rural scenario. We have already seen that in the traditional local self government of the tribal people, women had virtually no role; but now in the new Panchayats the tribal women are coming forward without any strong opposition from the communities concerned. This change is noticeable. Regarding non-tribal people in the PR system, most of them, including SCs are refugees from the erstwhile East Pakistan (now Bangladesh) and there was no such strong self-governing institutions in that society - hence, the change is certainly a welcome step.

The Constitution (73rd Amendment) Act, 1992 has come into effect from 24 April, 1993 as it received the assent of the President of India on 20 April, 1993. Tripura has already an Autonomous District Council for the tribal areas under the Sixth Schedule. The TTAADC has been excluded from the purview of the Constitution (73rd Amendment) Act as it was specifically mentioned in Article 234M, although it is also mentioned at the same time (234M - 4(b): "Parliament may, by law, extend the provisions of this Part to the Scheduled Areas and the tribal areas referred to in clause (1) subject to such exceptions and modifications as may be specified in such law, and no such law shall be deemed to be an amendment of this Constitution for the purposes of article 368." Thus the scope of extension to the TTAADC is there.

The TTAADC is the fruit of a long democratic struggle of the people of Tripura in which the tribals and the non-tribals were equal partners. In the history of the world, we have rare parallel instance where such a big number of non-tribal people came forward for the tribal cause. The TTAADC was first constituted in 1982 and thereafter under the Sixth Schedule in 1985. The TTAADC cuts across all the 3 districts of the State. As the vast area of the TTAADC is excluded from the Panchayat Act, the total area of the 3

Zilla Parishads under the PR system will be little over one-third of the State and Zilla Parishads will be extremely small entities unable to sustain either district level Panchayats or district level planning. Thus the concept of 'district' will be facing a lot of complicacies. Again, at the intermediate level, the blocks in Tripura consists of both the TTAADC and the non-TTAADC areas. As the Panchayat Samiti is only for non-TTAADC areas in the block, the TTAADC areas will have to be excluded from the block. Thus in the same district and block, one will have a three-tier PR system and the other a single-tier TTAADC. Due to the implementation of the Constitution (73rd Amendment) Act in the non-TTAADC areas, a popular movement has already started in the TTAADC areas for the immediate constitution of the Village Committees (like the Gram Panchayats). The revitalisation process of the PR institutions in Tripura has evoked considerable enthusiasm among all sections of the people and it would have its impact in the TTAADC areas.

As the real meaning of self-government is autonomy or government without outside interference and at the same time accountability, the Tripura State Government does not at present interfere in the TTAADC affairs; although the government should act as a monitoring authority. The powers, authority, responsibility of the Panchayats - as listed in the Eleventh Schedule (Article 243G) appended to 73rd Amendment - are indicative, though not exhaustive, the TTAADC authorities are not ready at present, in consonance with the 73rd Amendment, to extend one-third reservation of Village Committee seats to the women although there would be no opposition from any quarter for at least ten percent seats for Village Committee, under the TTAADC to the women. This is a welcome development. The TTAADC is closely observing the Eleventh Schedule; but everything depends on the success story of the new Panchayats under the 73rd Amendment as the success in one institution like the Panchayat would automatically help raising demand in other self-governing institution like the TTAADC. In fact, the demand for real democratic institution, more power, and entitlement should come from below rather than any endowment from above.

In British India, the term 'local self-government' was widely used since 1870 to describe the limited reforms introduced in local bodies like the municipalities (Agartala Municipality was also established in 1871), but as Nirmal Mukharji (*EPW*, April 2, 1994, pp. 789 ff.) has very beautifully analysed how even in independent India the concept of local government hardly advanced beyond its 1870 level in most of the States. The Prime Minister in his address in the Conference of Ministers/Secretaries In-Charge of Panchayats (July 3, 1993, p.5) has admitted that one of the major reasons which hampered the development of local self-government has been the absence of regular and periodic elections within a time-frame; hence, these institutions have had unstable tenures. However, an ordinance is now issued on the Nagar-Palika and the Municipality election would be held in consonance with the Constitution (74th Amendment) Act just after the Panchayat election.

In the light of the above discussion, let us now suggest the following:

(A) The commitment for the devolution of 'power to the people' depends on the nature of co-operation of both the Central and the State governments. A financially weak and rickety State government, in spite of its best wishes, cannot virtually help the healthy growth of any local self unit. Hence, special grants should be extended to all the States of North East India for this purpose. A weak State cannot make a strong Centre. The trend of over-centralisation in many matters has virtually marginalised the State governments and a simmering discontent is noticeable in the entire N.E. zone of the country. The recommendations of the Sarkaria Commission should be implemented immediately. The State government should be made financially sound to translate the ideas as outlined in the 73rd and 74th Amendment Acts into reality and meaningful; as the PR bodies are in the State list.

(B) The self-governing institutions can play a successful role in future if the causes of limited success in the past are properly analysed and the structure of the rural society, particularly the tribal society, is properly evaluated. The State government and the TTAADC may jointly undertake the task of codification of customary rules and practices of all the tribes of Tripura to have a proper idea of the traditional self-governing institutions in the tribal society. True, a wind of change is blowing in the hills, the age-old chieftaincy system is given good-bye in some cases, still an idea of the traditional and customary laws is urgently needed before undertaking any change in the power structure.

(C) Census authorities may be requested to publish data either on smaller units or habitations so that these can be compiled to find the population of Gram Panchayat or Village Committee or on the basis of Gram Panchayat or Village Committee to determine properly the ratio of reservation of seats for SC, ST etc.

(D) It is expected that the states would endow powers and authority to their respective Panchayats and local self units; but what is usually found in many parts of the country is otherwise. Without persistent pressure from below and constant people's movement, any State government may show reluctance regarding effective devolution of 'governmental' authority to the local self-government institutes. The 73rd Amendment virtually says nothing about how to enforce its provisions. So, an enforcement provision regarding devolution of power may be incorporated.

In fine, it may be said that when such a big number of women and those from the weaker section of the society are elected to the grass-root organisations of the rural society to shape their own destiny and exercise such an authority, as outlined in the 73rd Amendment of the Constitution, the societal and attitudinal changes which would follow would definitely be quite revolutionary.

References

1. B.P. Misra, *Socio-economic Adjustments of Tribals : Case-study of Tripura Jhumias*, People's Publishing House, New Delhi, 1976.

2. Debapriya Deb Barman, *Treatise on Traditional Social Institutions of the Tripuri Community*, Directorate of Research, Government of Tripura, Agartala, 1983.

3. W.W. Hunter, *A Statistical Account of Bengal*, Vol. VI, Delhi, 1973.

4. L.P. Vidyaarthi, *Dynamics of Tribal Leadership in Bihar*, Kitab Mahal, Allahabad, 1978.

5. K.D. Menon, *Report on Codification of Tribal Customary Laws, Rites and Land Usages Pattern of Tripura*, 1991, (mimeo.).

6. Mahadev Chakravarty, et al., *A Study on the Lushai of Jampui Hills in Tripura*, Directorate of Research, Government of Tripura, Agartala, 1987.

   The Tripura Tribal Areas Autonomous District Council and the Tribal Problems: A Perspective, Government of Tripura, Agartala, 1986.

7. Proceedings and Papers of the Conference of Ministers/Secretaries In-charge of Panchayats, July 3, 1993, Ministry of Rural Development, New Delhi.

8. The Constitution (73rd Amendment) Acts (As passed by the House of Parliament), 1993.

9. The Tripura Panchayats Act, 1993; The Tripura Panchayats (Conduct of Election) Rules, 1993; The Tripura Panchayats (Delimitation of Constituencies) Rules, 1993; Panchayat Department, Government of Tripura, Agartala, 1993.

4

Traditional Self-Governing Institutions Among the Hill Tribal Population Groups of Tripura

– P.K. Basu

Panchayati Raj is a system of local government by which the people in rural areas can take upon themselves the responsibilities for their socio-economic and cultural development. Basically, it is an arrangement of participation of people in the administration of local affairs. In this sense this arrangement is not new and alien to the people of Tripura. Tripura had, during more than a thousand years of princely rule, indigenous institutions of rural government at the grass-root level particularly among the hill tribes. The principles, practices and procedures of the system, however, varied from community to community. Nevertheless, they had certain broad similarities.

Tripura is the permanent abode of a number of 'Scheduled' tribes, besides an over-bearing population of non-tribals. According to the 1961 Census of India, the following tribes reside in Tripura:

1. Bhil, 2. Bhutia, 3. Chaimal, 4. Chakma, 5. Garoo, 6. Halam, 7. Jamatia, 8. Khasia, 9. Kuki, 10. Lepcha, 11. Lushai, 12. Mag, 13. Munda, 14. Noatia, 15. Orang, 16. Reang, 17. Santal, 18. Tripura or Tripuri, Tippera, and 19. Uchai.

Out of these nineteen Scheduled and recognised tribes all over the State of Tripura, only eighteen are listed and classified according to the information recorded in the individual Slips at the Census of 1971. No person has been found to have belonged to the 'Chaimal' tribe. The position remains the same in the Census Report of 1991 too.

It is to be mentioned in this connection that the tribes which are found in existence in today's Tripura might not have borne the same names and nomenclatures in the days of yore. There have certainly been permutations and combinations of the tribal populace throughout the ages. In fact, an honest endeavour has been made for the first time in the fifties of the last century through which classifications of different tribal communities have emanated.

An interesting point to be noted here is that out of the total nineteen listed Scheduled tribes of Tripura only eight tribes (Chaimal, Halam, Jamatia, Kuki, Noatia, Reang, Tripura and Uchai) may be called local Tripura tribes proper, since they are not known to have migrated from outside in the historical period like the others. Other tribes like Bhil, Munda, Orang and Santal (Central Indian Tribes) have come from Madhya Pradesh, Bihar, West Bengal and Orissa; Bhutias and Lepchas (Northern Frontier Tribes) have hailed from the northern frontier of the country (Bhutan, Sikkim, North Bengal); Garoo, Khasia and Lushai are said to be Assam Tribes; and the Chakmas and the Mogs have come from Chittagong Hill Tracts and the Arakans.[1]

Nature has been too lavish upon the State of Tripura in bestowing with recurring contrast of woodland and tillage, alteration of hills and villages, wood and river. The country life of the State is naturally calm, simple and unexciting. Most of the villages are far-flung and situated in the plain areas often disturbed by intermittent hills. Apart from the divisions within the tribal community whereby we come across a conglomeration of a variety of faith, language, religion, culture, etc., there has been the conspicuous presence of Bengali cultural heritage with its over-bearing impact. The Princely administration headed by the Tribal Maharaja was structurally tiny, numerically small and physically remote. It let the different tribal communities cultivate their respective cultural pursuits along with socio-religious heritages in their own improvised manner. The reason as to why the monarchical regime of Tripura did not want to hinder the growth of self-governing institutions including cultural pursuits of the tribal people in a direct manner may be best answered in the words of the then Dewan Bejoy Kumar Sen, the Chief Secretary of the *Tipperah State,* who said in 1917, while replying to the British allegation of loose administration in certain parts of Tripura, "It is an extensive and wild territory, full of deep forests, intersected with lofty ranges of hills, and interspersed with vast swamps. Necessarily its administration presented difficulties, and had to be carried on mainly through the agency of clan Chiefs, but it is hardly correct to say that the Durbar exercised no authority over it[2]."

Thus the administration wielded an overall administrative control over the local social structure of various tribal communities, while refraining from active interference in their institutional devices. This policy paid rich dividends as can be discerned in the statement of Sri Brajendra Datta, an employee of the Tripura Administration from 1897 to 1926 who stood witness to the non-tribal colonisation of Tripura. "It was easier to govern the tribes than the newcomer Bengalis—particularly the Muslims—because the tribals followed their customary laws and were loyal to their own tribal Chiefs; as a result, the Tripura Government had little to bother about them[3]".

The *Tripura Desher Katha*[4] written in 1724 by two Assamese envoys describes the skeleton administrative set up of a village called Rangrung situated in northern Tripura. The village was inhabited by about 300 people who were connected with the Maharaja of Tripura through their own *Sardar* called *'Halamcha'* under whom there was one *'ghalim'*, one *'gaboor'*, one *'chapia'* and one *'doloi'*. This description depicts an idea of the Maharaja's authority over the distant hills of Tripura. It also proves that the tribal villages enjoyed local autonomy under their age-old self-administrative system.

In later years the post of *'Missip'* was created for better administrative network. The *Missip* was engaged as a liaison officer between the Maharaja and the headman of a particular tribe. He was generally a trusted man of the Maharaja and was one of his kith and kin. B.P. Misra presents the nature of relation between the Maharaja and his tribal subjects in the following words.

'The individual tribal was the subject of the Maharaja and not of the *Sardar* or *Roy* of his tribe; but the tribe as a whole enjoyed much of freedom. This was so because the *Roy* or Headman of a tribe was treated as a subordinate King (Samanta Raja) by the Maharaja[5]'.

We may now have a look at the social hierarchical structure of the tribals of Tripura which presents an overall picture of elaborate self-governing institutions of various tribal communities of Tripura operating in their respective cultural atmosphere. It is to be noted in this connected that there has been a continual interplay of actions and reactions in these systems, as a result of which significant admixtures have been generated. Thus the original customs, manners, religious rituals and even local self-governing structures of different tribal sects have undergone various changes through an ever-flowing chain of intercourses.

Organisation of Village Council

In 1959 the Ministry of Home Affairs, Government of India, appointed a Committee to evaluate the working of what were then called Special Multipurpose Tribal Blocks. The Committee headed by the renowned anthropologist Verrier

Elwin was asked to examine, *inter alia,* the working of the traditional tribal councils. Selecting an area in the South of the State of Tripura, the Committee carried out its survey and observed.

'The people here live in small villages known as *Paras.* The *Para* has a traditional leader, the *Sardar,* who has considerable influence and under his guidance and control the communal activities of the villages are carried on. He is responsible for the observance of the customs and laws of tribal society. The traditional leadership is, however, disintegrating rapidly owing to external influence[6]'.

The Village (tribal) Councils in Tripura were informal in character, deriving their authority from tradition and antiquity. They were supported by social and supernatural sanctions. The date of selection, term of office and number of posts, etc., are not definitely known. Party politics was conspicuous by its absence. The Headman's house or *Kachari* was the premise for the purpose of administration. The office-bearers of the Council did not get formal salary. The headman did, however, enjoy certain privileges and services from the villagers.

Each Village Council consisted of a few office-bearers. The designations of a few tribal village officials may be cited here.

1. **Tripuri Village Council:** The *Kami-fang* or *Chaudhuri* or *Sardar* was the headman. The *Achai* or the *Ojhai* was the priest or sorcerer. The *Karpang* or the *Karbari* was the treasurer and Secretary. The *Khandal* was the peon and messenger.
2. **Halam Village Council:** The political structure of the Halams consisted of the *Kanskow,* the *Ghalim,* the *Gabor* and the *Rai* in the order. The *Rai* headed the court, which was the adjudicator in all criminal and civil matters. The *Rai,* appointed for a fixed tenure of

five years, was succeeded by the *Ghalim,* who was in turn succeeded by the *Gabor* and so forth. Each one of these functionaries was assisted by two volunteers, who were appointed in serial order in terms of existing rules and regulations. The volunteers in their turn became *Kansknows* and so on. All these functionaries used to work on behalf of their children, those having none being debarred from holding office.

3. **Jamatia Village Council:** The Jamatias, though they once belonged to the Tripuri tribe, managed to evolve a political system of their own. At the apex of their political hierarchy they had two functionaries, known as *Akra.* In their socio-political and administrative set-up, Tripura was divided into sixteen *mahals,* each under the charge of two *Panchais.* The *Panchais* were elected by all the village headman known as the *Chaudhuri* who in turn was elected by the people of the *Para* (village). There was no fixity of tenure for these posts. The incumbents used to continue to hold office as long as they could enjoy the confidence of the people. The *Akra* was the final authority for disposing of criminal and civil matters. Fines, physical torture including caning were often resorted to as punishment.

4. **The Riangs:** So far as the social administrative structures of the Riangs are concerned, they had first of all fourteen *dafas* or sections. Each *dafa* had its own administrative head. These heads were also the ex-officio members of the Government for the whole tribe. The list given on the next page, provides the designation of the heads of different *dafas.*

In all, they had twenty-seven administrative heads for the fourteen *dafas;* they had nineteen different designations. These heads together formed the central administrative machinery for the Riangs. The *Roy* was the King for the whole tribe, while the *Kachkau* acted as the minister to him.

Sl. No.	*Dafa or Section of the Riang Tribe*	*Designation of the Head of the Dafa*
1.	Tuimui	Roy and Karma
2.	Mursui	Chapia Khan Yakchung
3.	Mechka	Chapia and Yakchung
4.	Apei	Kachkan and Darkalim
5.	Charki	Kachkan and Daiya-Hajra
6.	Masa	Hajra and Kanda
7.	Rai Kachak	Doloi and Khaskalim
8.	Taqma Yakcha	Muria and Khaskalim
9.	Oaring	Daoa and Kangreng
10.	Nak - Qam	Karma and Dukaria
11.	Chameprong	Sengakrak and Khandal
12.	Sagaray	Bhandari and Hajra
13.	Riang	Kachkau
14.	Darbang	Karma and Kangreng.

The *Roy* and the *Kachkau* had again separate groups of people to serve under their direct supervision, the details of which are furnished below.

The Office of Roy

1.	Roy	The King of Riangs
2.	Chapia Khan	Prince, acts as Roy in his absence
3.	Chapia	The would be Chapia Khan
4.	Darkalim	Priest
5.	Doloi	Prosecutor
6.	Bhandari	Storekeeper
7.	Kanda	Attendant of Roy
8.	Daiya Hajra	Drummer
9.	Dukaria	
10.	Muria	Shehni - player
11.	Daoa	Assistant to Darkalim
12.	Sengakrak	Royal umbrella bearer

The Office of Kachkau

1.	Kachkau	Minister
2.	Yakchung	Treasurer
3.	Hajra	Attendant of Kachkau
4.	Kangreng	Umbrella bearer for Kachkau
5.	Karma	Attendant of Yakchung
6.	Khas Kalim	Umbrella bearer of Yakchung
7.	Khandal	In-charge of food supply.

The Lushais

To have a glimpse of the administrative structure within the Lushai society we find the Village Council at the apex of the political and economic life of the village. The Village Council had five to ten members, the number varying from village to village, though the two key functionaries were the President and the Secretary. The Council was elected every three years by all the members of the village who used to assemble in a central place and record their voice on a slip of paper. The Council enacted its own code of laws and meted out summary justice. The President was considered to be the 'de facto' arbiter of the economic destiny of the village. The Council used to act as the all-powerful authority in the village.

Next to the Village Council, there existed the family which was a very powerful social institution. The family, the base unit, engaged its attention to all sundries starting from marriage laws to the nature of economy prevalent within the society.

The Chakma

The top functionary of a Chakma Village was the *Karbari* whose primary duty was to collect rent and serve summons issued by the *Dewan* or the *Raja*. The Karbaris which in the past were appointed by the *Dewans* or *Talukdars* of the respective clans of a village, acted as the supreme authority in the village. The *Dewans* or the *Talukdars* of a village had to pay *nazar* (tribute) to the Raja for all of their omissions and commissions in revenue and judicial matters in which they were treated as the executive authority within the village. In between the *Dewan* and the *Karbari* there was a functionary known as the *Khisa* in case of a bigger clan. Even today these functionaries retain a great deal of their age-old power and glory and the experiment of village level democracy is tending to perpetuate it.

The Mags

The Mag society was ruled by *Bohmong, Chaudhury or Tehsildar*. The *Mags* used to solve their own disputes through their own social institutions and seldom, if ever, they had to take recourse to judicial process.

The Santals, Mundas and Oraons

These tribes, original settlers of Chota Nagpur region for centuries, came over to Tripura via Sylhet to work as labourers in the tea gardens. They led a closely-knit social life surrounding the village, the physical base. The society was dominated by the *Sardars*. The final court of appeal of the Santals was the Council of Fortyeight *Sardars* from different areas of Tripura known as the *Mandal*.

During the long period of princely rule, traces of any royal statue were indeed scanty. Acting on the instructions from the first Political Agent appointed by the British for improving the sort of anarchic, haphazard and autocratic style of administration in Tripura, the judiciary was for the first time separated from the executive department, more specifically from the hands of the King in 1872. In 1878 the *Pahari Adalat* which was created with its seat at the capital, was however, abolished with a view to establishing rule of law and introducing a uniform pattern of judicial administration for all categories of subjects.

With the passage of time the traditional Village Councils started showing massive disorganisation and decadence. It was in 1929 when the last ruling Maharaja of Tripura (Bir Bikram Manikya 1923 - 47) enacted a law known as *Tripura Khatriya Samaj Sankranta Niyamabali* to stem the rot. Of course, this law made significant departures from the traditional Panchayat. It sought to set up a uniform pattern of *Gramya Mandali* for all tribal villages and communities. It had also a wider jurisdiction than its predecessor. A word or two in this connection about some of the provisions of the Act of 1929 may not be irrelevant. For example, unlike its predecessor, the Act of 1929 clubbed together a number of contiguous hamlets to be looked after by a nominated body of nine elderly members who again were to be assisted by a team of ten young volunteers. Their term of office was three years. Furthermore, the system of paying a fee to the Council was institutionalised for the first time. Above all the *Gramya Mandalis,* a Central Committee consisting of twelve members and an Advisory Committee of three members were formed.

Death of the last ruling Maharaja (1947), partition of India, formal integration of Tripura into the Indian Union (1949), communal riots, massive influx of refugees from across the border, etc., all contributed to the shaking up and shattering the old set up in Tripura. The tribal life along with its old habit as well as habitat started changing on a faster pace, and their traditional Village Councils were exhibiting visible wear and tear. Even then in 1959 the Verrier Elwin Committee on Special Multipurpose Tribal Blocks recommended the recognition of the strong and alive Tribal Councils and revival of the Tribal Councils which had virtually fallen into disuse.[7] Speaking highly about the Councils, the Committee opined: The Tribal Councils have great potentialities. Established in history and tradition, supported by social and religious sanctions, expression of a genuine democracy representing the co-operative and communal temperament of the people, they can be used not only to support law and order but also to further the progress of development throughout the tribal areas.[8]

The Government of Tripura, however, failed to be convinced to take adequate steps in recognising or reviving the age-old tribal Village Councils. Instead, it adopted and introduced U.P. Panchayati Raj Act of 1947 in Tripura in 1959 for the entire territory. The first Left Front Government led by the Communist Party of India (Marxist), immediately taking up the reins of power in Tripura, demanded to the Government of India in 1978 introduction of the Sixth Schedule of the Constitution of India in the State with a view to constituting an effective and secured autonomous District Council for the tribal people. Its demand for the extension of the constitutional provision as applicable to the State of Assam, Meghalaya and Mizoram was, however, rejected by the then Janata Government at the Centre ostensibly because it would involve an amendment of the Constitution for which required majority in the Rajya Sabha might be wanting. Morarji Desai, then Prime Minister, accordingly advised the Left Front Government to make provisions for an ADC for the tribals of the state confining them within the limits of its constitutional power and authority. This meant the enactment of a law in this regard by the State Assembly by invoking the provisions of the Seventh Schedule [Article 246, State List, (3)] and the Fifth Schedule [Article 244(1)]. While the relevant provisions under the Seventh Schedule empower the State Legislature to enact laws for the creation of an ADC (creation of local government like Municipal Corporation, Improvement Trusts etc. - item No. 5 of the State List), the power to make adequate arrangements for ameliorating the conditions of the tribals of a State other than those protected under the Sixth Schedule has been incorporated in the Fifth Schedule. The Left Front, in the face of acute reality, adhered to the suggestions and prepared the ADC bill under the aforesaid constitutional provisions - thereby creating a unique model of experiment of self-governing institution ever witnessed before in the country.

The Tripura Tribal Areas Autonomous District Council constituted through election held in January 1982, worked under the aforesaid constitutional arrangement for about two and a half years, ultimately paved the way for the creation of such a Council under the Sixth Schedule of the Constitution in June 1985. Although the 'autonomy' part of the ADC under the first and the second constitutional scheme happens to be more or less the same, the vital question of survival of the ADC predominantly clinched the issue.* This arrangement salvaged some of the precious democratic characteristics of the age-old tribal Village Councils. And with the enactment of the Tripura Panchayati Raj Act of 1993 (in pursuance with the Seventy-third Constitutional Amendment Act) the three-tier Panchayati Raj Institutions (Zilla Parishad, Panchayat Samiti and Gaon Panchayat) were constituted through elections.

References

1. Misra, B.P., *Socio-economic Adjustments of Tribals, Case Study of Tripura Jhumias*, p. 3.
2. Sen, Dewan Bejoy Kumar, *The Eastern Boundary of the Tipperah State*, Appendix XX, p. 33.
3. Datta, Brajendra, *Udaypur Bibaran*, pp. 50-52.
4. Quoted from Gan Chaudhuri, J. (ed.), *Tripura, The Land and Its People*, p. 3.
5. Misra, B.P., *op. cit.*, p. 41.

* The ADC under the Seventh-Fifth Schedule can be abolished by an act of the State Assembly, while that under the Sixth Schedule requires a Parliamentary enactment for its abolition.

6. Elwin, V., *Democracy in NEFA*, Shillong, 1965, p. 1.
7. *ibid.*, p. 51.
8. *ibid.*, p. 49.

5

Traditional Self-Governing Institutions Among the Hill Tribal Population Groups of Nagaland

– *A. Lanunungsang Ao*

1. Introduction

The main objective of the paper is the describe the existing system of self-governing institutions among the hill tribal population groups of Nagaland and examine how far these self-governing institutions can offer an alternative to the present political arrangement.

It is strongly felt that the introduction of traditional system of self-governing institutions is the only answer to the Nagas, because the present political system which is an imposed one can never meet their political aspirations. The Nagas have lost their confidence on the people's elected representatives because of their failure to function efficiently under the alien system of 'democracy'. They are now demanding for an alternative solution. It is obvious that the present political arrangement cannot deliver the goods to the needy people. Therefore, it is felt imperative to reinstate the traditional system of self-governing rural institutions giving sufficient scope to the grass-root level organisation. As Rajiv Gandhi had said, "Give power to the people". Gandhiji also remarked, "True democracy cannot be worked out by twenty men sitting at the Centre.

It has to be worked out from below by the people of every village." Therefore, at this juncture it is felt that a kind of self-development management perspective ingrained in grass-root level institutions should be adopted.

2. Some Observations of the Outsiders

The British administrators were amazed to see the uniqueness of the Naga traditional system of government. Some of their observations are reproduced below:

> "Each village amongst the *Aos* is a small Republic. And each man is as good as his neighbour, in deed, it would be hard to find anywhere else more thoroughly democratic.[1] The least that can be said of the Nagas is that, in general they have mental outlooks and mental processes far more consistent with those of the Europeans and the ordinary natives of India.[2] Every Naga follows the dictates of his own will, a form of the purest democracy which it is very difficult indeed to conceive as existing even for a day, and yet that it does exist here, which is an undeniable fact.[3] First of all, a Naga by nature is one who is ever eager to know things. It is for this that he discusses problems first at home, then at the level of his clan, then in the meeting of the representatives of his entire tribe. At each level, anyone present has full freedom to express his views and to ask questions.[4] Coupled with democracy of the Nagas, there was the factor of independence of villages. These *Village States* were like Greek city states an image which British used at the time to conjure up as the height of civilization. In this way the Naga people were regarded as having a cultural nobility which was perhaps, one of the reasons that the Britisher excluded them from the hierarchical influence of the plains".[5]

It was in 1950-51, that Jairamdas Doulatram the then Governor of Assam, had given a very strong remark that "the Nagas should not be forced to practise the adult franchise system because it is against their well established tradition bound institution. Rather they should be encouraged to continue with their *Great Grand Tribal Council System* according to their own tradition". He further said that, "the minute they are forced to go with the Indian system of election, their society will be divided into pieces and their descent Naga tradition and their identity will disappear". This suggestion was highly appreciated by Jawaharlal Nehru, the then Prime Minister of India. Perhaps, these leaders could clearly visualise the evil consequences of the modern political party system upon the self-ruled tribal Naga society. What they had apprehended long ago, is now being experienced by the Nagas today.

In spite of very strong opposition and resentment launched by the Naga general public; even upto to the extent of boycotting the alien system of election in 1952, a Centre-sponsored state government was imposed in Nagaland on December 1, 1963. The Naga general public have now realised that this alien political structure should be completely dismantled to bring back the golden Naga traditional self-governing system.

3. Relevance of the Traditional Self-Governing System in Naga Society

There are several reasons as to why this traditional self-governing institution is relevant in the context of Naga society today. They are:

(i) Historical Reason

Since time immemorial the Naga village government was the only accepted government among the Nagas. There had never been a king or an emperor among the Nagas. (Even today, the Naga society represents a classless society). They ruled themselves, administered and managed the affairs for the independent Naga village republics by themselves without any outsiders' interference. Every citizen was just like a trained soldier and police personnel guarding and protecting the village. Every elderly person was like a Judge in a modern civil court. They love to continue with this kind of self-governing institution today to protect and preserve their tribal distinctiveness.

As a matter of the fact, the Nagas are not likely to accept any imposed system which is alien to their tradition. It is because of the imposition that they are going through a serious identity crisis.

When the British administrators and Christian missionaries landed in Naga Hills during nineteenth century for the first time, they were surprised to note the Naga democracy working at the highest level. From their records, it is evident that the traditional self-governing system was perfectly working in Naga society prior to the advent of the British. It was the village government which could manage the affairs of the villages in terms of safeguarding and promoting welfare schemes though the villagers were totally illiterate. Today, the villagers are much better educated. That is why we expect that they can manage their affairs much better than before, be in administration of justice or developmental programmes, once they are given a chance to do it.

(ii) The Naga Commune System

By and large the distribution of Naga population is based on distinct socio-cultural and geo-physical factors. The network of each tribal organisation is then based on more or less communal and corporate nature. The unique feature of each of the Naga tribe is the family, the clan, the village and the tribe forming into a community with strong sense of tribal solidarity. Each tribe is living within a given geographical area. Every tribe speaks different dialect, which is not understood by another tribe. Each Naga family, khel, village, range and area is well organised into a form of union, association, assembly (*hoho*). For instance, the *Aos* are scattered in six different ranges and in other growth centres of Nagaland. Their apex body of socio-political institution is called the "*Ao Senden Salang*". The *Lothas* are also living in the same pattern of geographical distribution. They are occupying three distinct ranges. The *Angamis* are living in four compact areas of Kohima district, the *Konyaks* are in three ranges of Mon district. The rest of the Naga tribes are also living in the same pattern of geographical distribution. Each of them is having a unified system of socio-cultural and political organisation with distinct boundaries; i.e. geographical, cultural, political, social, and economic etc. There is a high degree of socio-political cohesion and tribal solidarity within their community. Considering such existing social fabrics and potentials, an effective traditional self-governing system can be worked out by re-organising the existing rural social institutions.

(iii) Appropriateness of the Institutions

A three tier system of Panchayati Raj Institution (PR) as laid down in the 1992 Act is nicely fitting to Naga society because this kind of rural social institution had already existed there even before the introduction of local self-government in India. Village councils at village level, area councils at range level and tribal councils at the district level have been functioning. Considering the Naga commune system as mentioned in (ii) above, the operation of four tier system of Naga Hoho Model as proposed by the Naga Scholars' Society will be one of the answers not only to the Nagas but also to other hill population groups of the North Eastern Region of India.

(iv) The Opportunities of the Special Constitutional Provision for the Nagas

A tremendous change is likely to take place on Self-governing System in India after 73rd Amendment Act, 1992. This

Act reaffirms the objective of the democratic decentralisation and suggests that every state government should work out the structure of local self-government suitable to its local conditions. The Act provides more freedom to the operation of PRI in India. It does not in any way, encroach upon the jurisdiction of the states. Respective state governments are empowered to take appropriate decisions in conformity with the 73rd Amendment Act.

It is clear that this Amendment Act does not bind the state of Nagaland, because there is a special constitutional provision for the Nagas under Article 371(A). The Amendment Act of 1992 has clearly mentioned that it does not disturb the special constitutional provision for the state of Nagaland. Therefore, the state Nagaland can enjoy greater amount of opportunities of the traditional self-government under this constitutional provision which says: "Notwithstanding anything in this Constitution; no Act of Parliament in respect of:

(i) Religious or social practices of the Nagas;

(ii) Naga customary laws and procedures;

(iii) Administration of civil and criminal justice involving decisions according to Naga customary laws;

(iv) Ownership and transfer of land and its resources;

shall apply to the state of Nagaland unless the Legislative Assembly of Nagaland by a resolution so decides"

This is one of the outcomes of the Sixteen-Point Agreement reached between the Naga People's Convention (NCP) and the Government of India in 1960.

In Point 8, under Local Self-Government, it is stated that, "each tribe shall have the following units of rule making and administrative local bodies to deal with the matters concerning the respective tribes and areas : (1) the village council; (2) the range council; and (3) the tribal council. These councils will also deal with disputes and cases involving breaches of customary laws and usages". Point 9 of this agreement envisages the administration of justice (the Naga Tribunal for the whole of the Nagaland) according to Naga Customary Law. These constitutional provisions were made considering the Naga socio-political background in mind and these need immediate implementation. The Nagas in general and the state government of Nagaland are now seriously pondering to harness such opportunity by enacting appropriate laws. The above article opens enough scope for the Nagas to constitute self-governing institutions suitable to their needs. This may fulfil the objective of the introduction of traditional self-governing institutions among the hill tribal population groups of Nagaland in North East India.

PART - II

The Naga Hoho Model

Based on the above background, a model of "self-governing system" is proposed below with special reference to the Nagas of Nagaland.

The model is called the Naga Hoho Model, which means the Naga Peoples' Assembly or Parliament. The model seeks to restructure the total political organisation in the state. This indigenous Naga model was first developed by the Naga National Council (NNC) on the basis of age-old Naga traditional self-governing system. The model is divided into four levels. They are :

1. The Village level *Hoho* at every Naga village;
2. The Range or Area level *Hoho* at every defined area;
3. The District level *Hoho* in every district of Nagaland state; and

4. The State level *Hoho* as the apex body of *Hoho*.

A *Hoho* at any level will be responsible and accountable. The size of a *Hoho* will be determined by the people themselves. The members of a *Hoho* will be nominated by the people themselves according to their customs. The administration of justice will be largely taken care by the Naga courts at different levels, relating to both civil and criminal justice according to their customary laws and procedures. This model does away with the existing imposed and superficial political constituencies. It discourages the present system of adult franchise too because under this proposed model, this will not be necessary at all. It will bring back the golden Naga traditional system of self-governance to the forefront as a trust motivating spirit of political action. Planning and development processes will be taken care by the *Hoho* at different levels which will be empowered with greater amount of autonomy, i.e., finance, administration of justice, planning and implementation of socio-economic programmes. This will be thoroughly a self-managed and self-governed arrangement through active participation of the people at all levels. The budgetary provision will be directly made available with the tribal banks to be organised by themselves at different levels especially at the range and district level *Hoho* under the direct control of the Apex Tribal Bank in the state level *Hoho*; for proper and safer means of channelling funds.

In this integrated model, people's assembly becomes a living institution with permanance. First, it will be necessary to re-organise the people's *hoho* at village level, area and district level. Then the state level people's *hoho* has to be reconstituted by the representatives of every tribal *hoho* from the district level *hoho*. The present alien and imposed system of legislative assembly gets replaced by this integrated and federal representatives of people's *hoho*. The *illustration* of every *hoho*, the size of *hoho*, the method of nomination and also their powers and duties are discussed in brief here below:

(1) *The Village Hoho*

The village *hoho* will the basic unit and the foundation of this four-tier system of people's *hoho*. Every village *hoho* will be vested with certain autonomy with responsibility to initiate developmental activities according to villagers' needs, aspirations and traditions. The ideal size of a village *hoho* could be considerably larger in size so as to draw the maximum participation of people from each section of their society. For determining the size of *hoho*, in the village level, two important criteria may be kept in mind; such as the actual size of the population, households, and the number of clans, khels living in that particular village. Keeping such points in mind, it is suggested that a village level *hoho* may have 11-15 clan representatives in village below 200 population, 15-19 in a village having 200-449 population, 20-25, for a village having a population of 2000 and above. It has to ensured that every clan is well represented in every village *hoho*, every village in area *hoho* and every area hoho in the district level *hoho*, and again, every district *hoho* in the state level *hoho* with proportionate distribution according actual size of population, area and other socio-cultural characteristics.

The members of the village representatives will be nominated by the villagers according to their traditional way of nomination and selection of their leaders. Qualifications of a member will be fixed by the villagers themselves according to their customs followed for selection of a leader. The selection of leader should be based solely on their social practices and customary procedures as found in the history of the village republic system.

(2) *The Area Level Hoho*

The size of area level *hoho* will also be determined according to the size of population and the number of villages falling under that *hoho*. The Naga tribal people are living side by side within a given definite and well demarcated geographical area. This should be considered while deciding the size of an area *hoho*. It is proposed that one representative may be chosen for every 500 persons. But in case of a smaller village having less than 500 population, two or more small villages may be clubbed together for sending their representatives to the area level *hoho*. They are to be chosen by the nominated member of the village *hoho* from among themselves or anyone of the qualified persons form within the jurisdiction of that particular *hoho* circle. The same pattern may be followed while selecting representatives in the remaining *hoho*.

(3) The Tribal Hoho

It may have 25-35 nominated members which may be determined according to actual size of the population of that particular area. They are to be nominated by the members of the area level *hoho* from the jurisdiction of that particular tribal level *hoho*. This will be the most important *hoho* in terms of distribution of fund for development, supervision and guidance of the lower level within their jurisdiction.

(4) The State Level Hoho

The size of this *hoho* may be expanded having 65-75 tribal representatives from different tribal *hohos* in the state. They have to be the selected members by the tribal *hoho* members. In this apex body of people's representatives, different categories of people are to be well represented such as the people from the farming group, the women group, the student population, retired personnel, professional group, academic and others; particularly in the state and tribal level *hohos*. The members of representatives are to be nominated normally for a term of 5 years with provision for renomination for another 2 years on the basis of their individual contribution and performance. One third of the members are to be replaced after every 2 years in every *hoho* of different levels. Thereby, every *hoho* remains as permanent rural social institution at different levels. The general public may be empowered to call back any of their representative form the *hoho* on account of misconduct, corruption, incapability and misrepresentation of the people. Such person may be disqualified by the people in every house and be replaced by new members immediately. The Chairman is to be selected by the members from among themselves for a period of five years in every *hoho*.

(5) The Town Hoho

In the urban areas, the same principle of rural *hoho* system could be conveniently worked out. In every town, tribal *union* or ethnic *hoho* may be constituted in the light of the above *hoho* system. From such community *union*, representatives to the town *hoho* may deputed. The nominated or selected members representing different blocks, sectors or khels shall form the Urban Hoho in every recognised town. From such urban *hoho*, they may send their nominees to the tribal and state level *hoho* for bringing rural-urban relationship and integrated approach to development, creating sound political and socio-cultural communication.

Under this model the responsibilities of planning and developmental activities are vested with the *hohos* at different levels. Development of art and culture, science and technology, education, economy, literature, industries, transport and communication system etc. are to be taken care by the *hohos* at different levels.

These independent people's *hohos* may seek affiliation, registration and recognition of other international level organisations for the purpose of economic and socio-cultural development. Under this system, a mechanised tribal clan-collective and joint farming system can be introduced within every *hoho's* jurisdiction.

Why this model is required?

There are many reasons as to why this model is required:

(1) This is the Naga way of indigenous traditional self-governing system;

(2) It is obvious that the present political set up cannot deliver goods to the people and it can never meet the needs and aspirations of the people;

(3) The present political structure and its system is an alien one imposed upon the Nagas against their will.

(4) All peoples have the right of self-determination. By virtue of that right they freely determine their political status and freely pursue their economic social and cultural development.[6]

Many scholars, political thinkers, social workers, planners and Naga general public are of the opinion that the most significant hindrance to economic development is the inappropriateness of the present system of state-sponsored elections on the Naga society. The Naga citizens, therefore, imperatively feel that first of all, the imposed political structure must be changed to bring back the golden Naga traditional political structure; modifying it to accommodate for changing needs.

This is indeed a controversial model at this juncture. Different political ideologies are emerging among the Naga leaders representing different political organisation or parties. Another pertinent question is how can it be operable in Nagaland within the ambit of Indian constitution? In fact, a thorough legal study may be required to examine whether this model could be accommodated as an alternative political arrangement for the Nagas; taking into account their socio-political needs and aspirations.

Notes and References

1. Verrier Elwin, *The Nagas in the Nineteenth Century,* Oxford University Press, 1961 London, p. 423.
2. Hutton, J.H., *The Angami Nagas,* London, Macmillan, 1921, p. 28.
3. Elwin, V., *op. cit.,* p. 525.
4. Elwin, V., *op. cit.,* p. 6.
5. Andrew Gray (ed.), *The Nagas and Nations and its Struggle against Genocide,* 1986, p. 46.
6. See International Covenant on Economic, Social and Cultural Rights of the Indigenous People, adopted by U.N., General Assembly Resolution 2200 (XXI) of 16 December, 1966. It came into force from 3 January 1976 in accordance with article 17; in which Indian Government was one of the leading countries with strong force to include the term *'SELF-DETERMINATION'* of the indigenous people as Human Rights. This has reference of Part I, article of the above Covenant.

6

Traditional Self-Governing Institutions Among the Tribal Groups of Mizoram

– *L.B. Thanga*

The Mizos and their allied ethnic groups constitute around 95.00 per cent of Mizoram's population.[1] They had strong an age-old traditional system of local self-administration of chieftainship. In a study of the traditional self-governing institutions among the hill tribal population groups of Mizoram, therefore, we will be concerned with the system of chieftainship amongst the Mizo and allied groups all of whom claim descent from the legendary cave called *Chhinlung*, also spelt sometimes *Sinlung*, having the same culture, tradition, customary law including marriage, inheritance and all animists before Christianity swept the North East from the latter part of the 19th century.[2]

The name *Mizo* itself had often been wrongly interpreted, even by some educated Mizo youths, as *Hillman* which is absolutely misconceived and wrong amounting to the extent of derecognising a distinct tribal entity whereas there have always been a large number of tribals of Tibeto - Burman origin collectively and variously known as Zo, Mizo, or Zomi in Mizoram; Kuki, Thado, Halam or Paite in Manipur and Tripura; Chin, Halka, Hualngo, Kachin in Myanmar; and Maru, Lisho, Sho/Asho or Lasi in the Arakans of Bangladesh and Myanmar.[3] It is customary with all these groups of tribals to name their clans after one of their forefathers. As such, the clan names given above are only illustrative and not at all exhaustive.

Like all other tribes not only in the north east but also elsewhere in the country, the Mizos have no written record of their ancient past; and what they know today about themselves are transmitted to them by words of mouth from their forefathers, from folk tales, legends, ballads, rituals and monuments still traceable both in Mizoram as well as outside beyond the international borders.[4] All the Mizo historians agree that their ancestors had left their original habitats in China many centuries ago; migrated southwards to Myanmar about four/five centuries ago; and finally came to their present habitats in Mizoram, Manipur, Cachar Hills and Tripura, and further to the west in the Arakans of Bangladesh in a series of movements during the 15th and 16th centuries.[5] The most distinguishing feature of the Mizo groups of tribals was that they always had a strong system of chieftainship through the ages. It was in this manner that Zahmuaka, the progenitor of the Sailo Chiefs of later years, became a Chief when the Mizos were still at Seipukhur in the then Burma in the middle of the 16th century[6]. When the British came and occupied the Mizo country, all the powerful Chiefs in Mizoram and those who offered resistance to the British were descendants of Zahmuaka and the land they annexed was called Lushai Hills instead of Mizo Hills. Throughout the period of their rule over Mizoram, the Britishers refused to acknowledge the correct name and identity of the people for the furtherance of their policy of 'divide and rule', the watchward of the British administration in India.

Every Mizo village was an independent entity and the Chief was sovereign and monarch of all he surveyed. Though the boundaries of the villages were never defined, there were never any case of boundary disputes. However, this was the age of 'might is right' and 'survival of the fittest.' Threat or actual pressure from the more powerful neighbouring Chiefs often led to abandonment of old villages for new village sites. Grabbing of other's land solely for adventure was not know but to preserve what they held was sacrosant.[7] Originally the Mizo villages were formed of closely-knit families and clans. With increase in population diversification of the family components followed, and this in turn led to the realisation of the need for a strong and solid system of administration within the villages. It is salutary that the Sailo as well as Chiefs belonging to other clans evolved and followed similar system of administration through a well-established council of elders. Whatever systems of levying tributes the Chiefs had, in recognition of their position over the lands the villagers occupied and cultivated, were made and executed through this council of elders as would be seen from the succeeding paragraphs.[8] This is also true in respect of other dues/ levies the Chiefs realised from their subjects.

From ancient past, in the life of a Mizo the Chief was all in all. Everything in the life of the village revolved round the Chief and his house. At the same time, the sense of fraternity and equality was the evident among the Mizos. The experience of Lt. Col. T.H. Lewin, one of most understanding and successful British officers in the administration of the hill tribals, elucidly described this spirit when he wrote, "on his visit to a Lushai village in 1866 he found a drunken villager behaving very freely with the Chief. Asked for an explanation of such disrespect being permitted, the Chief replied, 'On the war path or in the council, I am the Chief and my words are obeyed; behaviour like that would be punished with death. Here in the village, that drunkard is my fellow and equal"[9]. Continuing Lewin described the Lushai (Mizo) society as the realisation of the dreams of Plato, Bacon, and Comte and said, "Among the hill tribes we find an actual existing system in practical working, which might well be classed among the visions of Utopian Philosophy. Their mode of government may be described as a democracy tempered by disposition. The right of rule is hereditary, that is only men descended from a certain family can be Chiefs. It does not however follow that all members of this ruling race should be Chiefs; on the contrary, it is only those who are specially gifted and endowed with the capacity of drawing men to them who become so. A Chief's power is measured by the number of his fellows, and as the people who follow him are perfectly free agents, it is natural sequence that the fittest or sometimes the most fortunate, is the most powerful"[10]. Normally, the Chief would give his son a certain number of households on his marriage with which the son would set up a village of his own. He was not required to pay any tribute or any other form of dues to his father, but was expected to help one another in times of hardship or quarrels with other Chiefs. The youngest or the eldest depending upon the clan to which a Chief belonged would remain with the Chief to succeed him and all his property on death.

In the administration of his domain, the Chief was assisted by two important institutions, namely- (1) the Council of Elders, called *Upa* in Mizo, and (2) the *Zawlbuk*, the youngmen's dormitory. A *Upa* in the Chief's Council was not necessarily required to be elderly or aged as the term *Upa* would imply. Moreover in the pre-British and post-British period also, the life span of a Mizo was barely fifty years or even less, and the head of a family in a village at the age of thirty or even less could qualify for appointment as *Upa* in the Chief's council.

There was also no limit to the numbers of elders to constitute the council. The discretion was entirely with the Chief. The Chief would normally appoint *Upas* as representatives as possible form different clans/ families in his village. Moreover there was no financial involvement in the appointment of *Upas;* and since the office was held for a life time, more by way of convention than by rule, the numbers of the council of elders varied from village to village and were never too few. In those days, the only means of exchange was by barter, and the *Upas* were compensated for their services by way of preference in the selection of jhum sites which otherwise were the prerogatives of the *Ramhuals* and *Zalens* about whom we shall discuss subsequently. In all festivals and other important functions in the village, the *Upas* were also given the position of honour next only to the Chiefs and in that way they occupied higher position in the society even though the Mizo society was basically classless. The frequency of the meetings of the council of elders was not fixed and the council of elders were required to meet as often as required and at any hours of the day or night.

The functions of the council were mainly judicial and executive. In the absence of any other authority the council members were also required to evolve principles or practices for the community, if well-established customs were not prevalent. In other words, they were expected to function as the legislative authority. Needless to say, in all these executive, judiciary and legislative functions, their authority was supreme and the Chief seldom questioned the wisdom of the decree of the council of elders. However, in the exercise of judicial powers there was never any case of capital punishment being imposed.

Whenever the council of elders met for business on any matters, a contribution known by the name of *Salam* meaning a fee for feast, was collected to feed the council members. As the Mizo society was comparatively liberal with fairly free mixing among the youth belonging to opposite sexes, a large number of cases coming up before the council for adjudication were those relating to marriages, divorces and others arising out of sexual offences and licenses. Normally, therefore the *Salam* was realised from the party found at fault in the dispute, unless otherwise specifically decreed by the council of elders. Very rarely disputes were settled other than by a consensus in which case the *Salam* was equally shared by both parties to the disputes.

The other important function of the council of elders was the allocation areas for jhum cultivation annually. The council members were the ultimate authority in this and the Chief rarely ever questioned the wisdom of the council in this regard. In this business, however, the council was always guided entirely by the advice of the *Ramhuals* and the *Zalens* who were selected and subsequently approved by the council of elders from the progressive affluent farmers in the village capable to come to the aid of the Chief himself or any other families in the village during distress. In recognition of this position, the *Ramhuals* and the *Zalens* were given along with the members of the council of elders the right of first choice in the selection of jhum fields annually. Moreover, the *Ramhuals* and the *Zalens* were required to pay higher quantity of *Fathang* (paddy tax) to the Chief. The positions of *Ramhuals* and *Zalens* were held during the pleasure of the Chief, and unless they themselves declined to continue holding the positions for any reason, they were normally held for a life time and could be inherited by the male children. Here also the numbers of *Ramhuals* and *Zalens* were not fixed and normally depended on the size of the village households. No wonder, in the practical working of the village administration through the council of elders by the Chief, T.H. Lewin classed the Mizo system among the classic vision of Utopian Philosophy in practice.

In this system of administration, the task of the Chief was doubly strengthened by the system of youngmen's dormitory system referred to earlier as the *Zawlbuk*. I had written at some length about this institution in my book *'The Mizos – A Study in Racial Personality'*.[11] I had mentioned that the origin of this institution is now lost in oblivion. However, it appeared that this system of youngmen's dormitory came into being after the Mizos migrated west from Burma. *Zawl* means a flat ground and *Buk* means a temporary rest hut. Thus a *Zawlbuk* in a village meant a rest house in the most central flat place of land in the village used mainly for public gathering, for festivities or any other purposes including religious functions. It was therefore usually built close to the Chief's house. In a very big village of more than a couple of hundred houses, there could be more than one *Zawlbuk,* but in such cases also the one nearest to the Chief's house would be the main one from where all the others would receive guidance and instructions.

A *Zawlbuk* served many purposes. In olden days when the villages were constantly at war with one another, the youngmen in the village would all sleep together in the *Zawlbuk* so that in case of any emergency, they could be marshalled together quickly. The building was not constructed in the way an ordinary dwelling house in a Mizo village is built. There were no windows or doors. A small opening in the front served as a door with a long unhewn log of timber serving both as a door over which one had to stoop double and pass through it by crawlling over the log. Another opening at the back with no shutter served as a window.

A fire was burnt in the *Zawlbuk* all the hours of the day and night and the supply of fuel for the hearth was the responsibility of all the boys in the village. As soon as the boy could prove that he had come of age, he was exempted from this labour, and such occasion would be a matter of great joy, for the boy could then be regarded as having attained the age of puberty and could take part in wars. Here all the youngmen of the village would collect together after the evening meals, and later call on their girl friends for gossip, smoke, or plan for the next day's work through *Inlawm,* which is a form of co-operative efforts of voluntary contribution of labour in exchange of labour primarily in the jhum fields but could be extended for other types of barter in labour. The elderly persons of the village would also gather every night to exchange news of the day and only retire when the youngmen would, one by one, return to sleep for the night. All visitors from other villages having to spend a night in the village had to take shelter and sleep in the *Zawlbuk* and not in the houses of the persons with whom they had taken shelter as guests. Here the youngmen of the village would put them to all types of trial of strength, the most popular being wrestling, so that the visitors could be made to feel at home in a strangers' land.

When the British came and took over administration of the Mizo country, they found the Chief and his council of elders and the *Zawlbuk* a very convenient institution. The entire fabric of a Mizo life in the village, social, cultural and even religious revolved round the *Zawlbuk* life. In course of time, however, with the stabilisation of the administration and less and less of inter-village strifes and quarrels, side by side with the establishment of schools at least at the primary levels, it was becoming more and more difficult to gather enough boys to maintain the hearths in the *Zawlbuk*. N.E. Perry and A.G. McCall, the district administrators in 1924-28 and 1935-43 respectively tried their best to uphold and preserve this *Zawlbuk* institution, even by an executive order.[12] As such, this important pillar of village administration and one of the most effective instruments to assist the Chief in his day to day administration began to decline nearly two decades before the dawn of independence; and by the time the move to abolish chiefship in Mizoram gained momentum soon after independence, there were no more *Zawlbuk* except as relics of history in few villages.[13]

With respect to the chieftainship and the institution of the council of elders to help the Chiefs in the administration of their villages, during the period of fifty seven years of British rule, the position of the Chiefs was not only consolidated but their numbers increased considerably. When R.B. McCabe in charge of North Lushai Hills District during 1887-1892 counted the population under his charge, he found only 25 villages with 8,318 houses and 41,590 population.[14] When the first census in Mizoram was conducted in 1901, there were 239 villages with 82,434 population. There was no separate counting of the number of Chiefs. It was, however, known that most of the Chiefs and their regents ruled over two villages or more. When N.E. Perry undertook codification of the Mizo customary laws and consulted as many Chiefs as possible to make his monograph on the customary laws as authentic as possible, he could find 46 Chiefs belonging to Sailo, and 10 belonging to other clans - a total of 56 Chiefs in all. This was in 1927. In 1954, that is 27 years later, when the rights and privileges of the Chiefs were abolished throughout the length and breadth of Mizoram, there were 309 Chiefs of whom 169 belonged to the Sailo and the remaining 140 belonged to other clans[15].

In addition to the Chiefs and the members of his council of elders, the other important functionaries in the old Mizo village were (1) the Village-Crier, *Tlangau* in Mizo, (2) the Blacksmith (*Thirdeng*), (3) the Priests (*Puthiam*) of which there were always two types, namely (a) the Priest who officiated in all religious functions and (b) the Priest who was required to propitiate evil spirits in the event of sickness or any other occasions where evil spirits were believed to be the mischief-makers.

None of the above functionaries were expected to have any time for cultivation. In recognition of their services to the villagers, therefore, each household was expected to donate a measure of paddy, which was not uniform and differed from village to village. In the case of the village blacksmith, he was also entitled to a share of a meat if a wild animal was killed by a hunter, but not when caught in a trap.

Prior to the occupation of the Mizo country by the British, there was no system of any collection of cess or tax by the Chief in recognition of his sovereignty over his land. However, what might be called an equivalent of land revenue in the form *Fathang,* that is paddy-tax, was collected from each villager. The *Fathang* for the ordinary villager and the *Fathang* for the Ramhuals and the Zalens were not the same, the quantity payable by the Ramhuals and the Zalens being almost the double of what the ordinary villagers paid. After the British came, and uniform rate of *Fathang* was introduced throughout Mizoram.

In addition, a Chief collected two other types of taxes, namely (a) *Sachhiah* (meat tax) and (b) *Chi-Chhiah* (salt tax). The first was the share of any animals reared at home, or killed in the forest, for which the hind right leg of the animal was the share of the Chief as the sovereign owner of the land. *Chi-Chhiah* was not common as it was seldom that a salt spring was located, but the few such fortunates were liable to pay the tax to acknowledge that the Chief was the owner of all that could be extracted from the land. The British did not introduce any new system of levy or tax but continued to recognise what had been practised earlier. They should be complimented for not introducing a complex system of land revenue accept simple house tax[16].

In addition to the above recognised form of dues payable to the Chiefs, the villagers had, by tradition and convention, to render various forms of voluntary services to the Chiefs in return for his role as the guardian and protector of the village. The most common one of such voluntary services rendered to the Chiefs was the construction of the Chief's house entirely free of cost. In course of time, the needs of the Chiefs and their desire to improve the standard of living began to increase resulting in the increase in the burden of impressed labour demanded from the villagers. Along with this was the increasing demand from the government for free labour to facilitate the movements of the government employees in the discharge of their duties when visiting villages. On the other hand, the government had to give recognition to those who had rendered uncommon services, e.g. such persons recruited to help the government in quelling the 'Abor Revolt' in 1911-12 and the World War I offered complete exemption from the 'Impressed Labour' popularly called *'Coolie'* duty. By such processes, a form of class system entirely unknown to the Mizo society was introduced. In short, the chieftainship in Mizoram was not only perpetuated and consolidated by the British but novel, if not entirely evil, innovative practices were introduced not to the liking of the people.

The movement for the abolition of chieftainship in Mizoram on the eve of independence which gained tremendous momentum soon after independence and the actual abolition of the age-old system in 1954 is to be understood in this context. This movement was closely linked with the demand for district autonomy embodied in the Sixth Schedule of the Constitution itself. The autonomy movement in the North East including the one in Mizoram itself is a subject-matter worthy of independent and full-fledged study. For our present study, suffice it to mention that the system of village councils in the erstwhile autonomous district council areas of Mizoram replacing the traditional chieftainship was somewhat novel to the Mizos though closely similar with the practical working with the system of the council of elders under the Chiefs. Since we are presently concerned with the traditional self-governing institutions of the tribals, a study of the village council system could be said to be almost irrelevant. However, it is now over fifty years old at least in Mizoram. Since the village council system in Mizoram was constituted, as mentioned earlier, in the model of the defunct council of elders under the Chiefs, it could provide useful guidance for the proposed Panchayati Raj system under consideration.

Any student of the political history of our country is aware of the origin of the Sixth Schedule of the Constitution providing District Autonomy to the hill districts of the former state of Assam. The district autonomy evolved was the handiwork of the Bordoloi Committee and when the report of that Committee was discussed in the Constituent Assembly, opinions were sharply divided. One member went to the extent of saying, "To vest wide political powers in the heads of tribals is the sure method of inviting chaos, anarchy and disorder throughout the length and breadth of the country. I am not in favour of self-determination. The principle of self-determination has worked havoc in Europe. It led to the vivisection of India, arson, loot, murder and the worst crimes upon women"[17]. Similar apprehensions were expressed by other speakers.

Dr. B.R. Ambedkar, the Chairman of the Drafting Committee of the Constitution, completely defended the proposal to create autonomous district councils in the North East. He emphasised the difference between the tribals of the North East and other places pointing out that the latter have been more or less Hinduised and assimilated by the culture and civilisation of the people with whom they lived. This was not the case with the hill tribes of the North East who, having their own roots, culture and civilisation, have not adopted the mode of life and manners of their neighbours. He specifically pointed out that their laws of inheritance, marriage and customs were fundamentally different from those of the people of the plains. Dr. Ambedkar had sounded a note of warning to guard against separatist movement by pointing out that autonomy which simply meant self-government must go side by side with inequality in economic fields. To quote, "In politics we will have equality and in social and economic life we will have inequality. We must remove this contradiction at the earliest possible moment or else, those who suffer from inequality will blow up the structure of political democracy which this Assembly has so labouriously built up[18]". Obviously, the warning of Dr. Ambedkar was not taken note of sufficiently by the powers that be.

"The movements for autonomy generating through the pre-independence decades, finally culminated with the attainment of Indian Independence. The District Council status in 1952, the abolition of chieftainship and its replacement by Village Councils, representation in the provincial legislature, change in the name from *'Lushai'* to that of 'Mizo' were some of the historic developments witnessed by Mizoram in the immediate post-independence decade. In this, the role of the Mizo Union was undisputed in the rise of Mizo nationalism as was the case with the Indian National Congress in the rise of Indian nationalism.

"It may be recalled that the demand of the Mizo Union in the Bardoloi Committee was for complete self-autonomy in all subjects except foreign affairs, defence, currency and communications. In fact, what the Mizo Union wanted was a truly federating Union of India in letter and a spirit. Therefore, the District Council status was just a means, not an end, towards more autonomy."[19]

It was during the transition from the days of the Chiefs with his council of elders to the operation of the autonomous district and regional councils with the village councils at the base that the meaning of autonomy as understood at different levels began to cause pinpricks and heart-burning. Autonomy in political parlance which could simply mean a form of self-government, free from external interferences, began to have different meanings not easily comprehensible to a simple tribal mind. Autonomy was becoming more and more confusing. The aspirations of the Mizos for a share in the administration began to be questioned. After the formation of the Lushai Hills Autonomous District Council on 25th April, 1954 and of the Pawi-Lakher Autonomous Regional Council on 23rd April, 1953, the people found that the District Council's power to use 'Service Stamps', the use of government rest houses/circuit houses by the members of the District Council/Regional Council and similar other matters were being questioned by government offices. A legal battle whether the Governor of the state was empowered to deal directly with the District Council or only on the advice of the Council of Minister nearly stalled the functioning of the District Council.[20] The state government of Assam was accused of being casual and lackadaisical in its response to these issues.

To make matters worse, even before the Mizo Autonomous District Council completed its second term, an event of significant consequence, namely the flowering of bamboos followed by severe famine, overrun Mizoram in 1959-60. According to Mizo historians such an event takes place regularly at an interval of every fifty years, and voluntary organisation like the YMA as also the Church had warned the government to take precautionary and preventive relief measures. The Government of Assam was then busy with its Official Language Act with all its disastrous uprisings. The dominant political party of Mizoram, the Mizo Union, always a friend and follower of the Assam Government, was disillusioned because help was forth coming too late for the people of Mizoram and the party being in power had to bear all the blame. This in turn helped the rise of the MNF phenomenally.[21]

Election to the first District Council was held in February, 1952; the second in 1957 and before it could complete its term in June, 1962, the above mentioned famine had come and gone. In the first election in 1952, the Mizo Union had wrested all but one seat of the District Council whereas in 1957, it captured eleven only, the remaining eight were won by the *UMFO, Zalen* as it was locally known. The famine of 1950-60 gave new breadth of life to the Mizo Union and when third election to the District Council was held in February, 1962 the Mizo Union recaptured 15, the remaining five being shared by independents and the *EITU*, a successor to the *UMFO*.[22]

By virtue of para 3(e) & (f) of the Sixth Schedule to the Constitution, the District Council had powers to establish

Village Councils; and the Lushai Hills District (Village Council) Act, 1953 and the Pawi-Lakher Autonomous Region (Village Councils) Act, 1954 were duly framed. These Village Councils play a key role in Mizoram politics. It could be said without any fear of contradiction that whosoever controls the Village Councils controls Mizoram. Village Councils could be constituted as under :

For villages not exceeding 60 houses, 5 members

For villages between 61 and 100 houses, 6 members

For villages between 101 and 140 houses, 7 membeers

For villages between 141 and 180 houses, 8 members

For villages between 181 and 220 houses, 9 members

For villages between 221 and 260 houses, 10 members

For villages 261 houses and above 11 members

For the total number of members of the Village Council as determined above, one-third or nearest can be nominated by the Executive Committee of the concerned District Council and the rest elected by adult franchise in accordance with the rules framed by the District Council under this Act. For example, a Village Council with 11 elected members could have 3 or 4 nominated members; 10 elected members could still be given by the Executive Committee 3 or 4 nominated members. And herein lies the root of corruption for the party in power.

Only a member of Scheduled Tribes could be a member of the Village Council and he must have attained the age of 25 years, and be a registered voter. One can be a member of only one Village Council, and must a resident of the constituency from which he seeks election.

The term of the Village Council is three years extendable or reduced for a period not exceeding six months. There is also a provision for the dissolution of the Village Council on the plea of inefficiency the yardstick for the measurement of which again is at the discretion of the party in power, another possible root of corruption. A member who continuously absents himself from ten consecutive meetings of the VC may be declared to have vacated his seat; and election to fill the vacancy held after giving him opportunity to explain his absence.

A Village Council has a President and a Vice President appointed from amongst the elected members. Further an elected member is not to be appointed as the Secretary. He is to be appointed by the Government and he holds office at the pleasure of the Government. The President may, at any time, resign in writing to the Executive Committee of the District Council or to the government; but continues in office until his resignation is accepted. The Vice-President in turn submits his resignation to the President.

Besides the Secretary, another officer provided in the Village Council Act is the *Tlangau,* a village - crier who announces all the decisions of the Village Council. He is paid a salary. In addition he enjoys some privileges such as exemption from *Hnatlang,* a form of common service for the community for the common good of the villagers. He, like the Secretary, attends the meetings of the Village Council but has no right to vote. All the members of the Village Council are paid salaries the scale of which varies from council to council, and from time to time.

Elections to the Village Councils were held for the first time in June, 1954. It was contested by the Mizo Union, the UMFO and some independents. The Mizo Union won 86 per cent, the UMFO 10 per cent, and the Independents 3.54 per cent. There were complaints of rigging by the MU. They were referred to a Reviewing Committee which made certain recommendations; these were not accepted by the MU. The UMFO launched a non-cooperation movement which induced the MU to the path of reason. Thus the fact remains that the first general election to the Village Councils was not free and fair.[23]

Election to the second Village Councils was duly held in 1957. The Mizo Union had split and they could win 66 per cent of the seats only, a reduction of 20 per cent from the first election. Even this election was not free and fair, and re-elections were conducted in a number of villages. The third, fourth and fifth elections could also be held duly and more or less on time in 1960, 1963 and 1966 respectively though suppression of some Village Councils on one ground or another had become more and more frequent in the intervening periods. It should also be noted that the fifth general election to the Village Councils in 1966 was disturbed by the outbreak of insurgency by the MNF. At the same time, the Village Councils were the most important machineries to assist the armed forces in their campaigns against the militants. Therefore, election or no election to the Village Council, the system was kept alive by keeping the Village Councils who had already outlived their term of office, by nomination of members to fill up the vacant seats and by any other means to keep the Village Councils functional. The next general election to the Village Councils after 1966 could be held only in 1971. The number of Village Councils decreased by 158 numbers because of the regrouping of villages as measures of both security and planned development. It was from this period that the period of proliferation of political parties in Mizoram had began, and at each new election one or another new party could be seen in the field, the result of which has been the gradual dominance of the national party, namely the Congress(I). We had already noted the powers of the Government to dissolve the Village Councils, and when done, they are always invariably on account of alleged corruption, financial mismanagements, incompetence, non-cooperation with the Government, favouritism; but almost all of which, if not totally, are the result of political manipulations.[24]

Of the three functions of the Village Councils listed in section 8 of the Village Council Act, 1953, the most important is the one relating to the allotment of jhum plots annually to the individual villagers, and such allotment/distribution of jhum plots is to be made in accordance with the laws/regulations made by the District Council for the purpose. It is in the exercise of this power that we now see the rise of an elite class of people similar to what are known elsewhere in the country as absentee landlordism. Side by side with this, they have power for allotment of house sites to the villagers, preservation of forest reserves, collection of land revenue and taxes, sanitary administration of the villages including prevention and outbreak of fires, communicable diseases; and above all, administration of justice including imposition of punishment equivalent to the powers of a third class magistrate but without limit in cases of disputes of civil nature. The strength of the village council courts varies from village to village as the members of the councils are the members of the courts concurrently. Offences of petty nature and all those falling within the purview of tribal and customary laws are triable by them. In cases, however, where the parties in the disputes belong to non-tribals, the village courts are barred from taking cognisance of the same. Appeals from the village courts lie to the Subordinate, Additional Subordinate, if there is one, or to the District Council court within a time frame prescribed in the rules.[25]

The Subordinate and the Additional Subordinate District Council Courts have jurisdiction over cases triable by the village courts in which both the parties to the dispute do not reside within the jurisdiction of the same village court. Subordinate District Courts are established in all the district headquarters while Additional Subordinate District Courts have now been established at important Sub-Divisional headquarters like Champhai. The District Council Courts is a court of appeals, and all appeals from the District Council Court lie to the Gauhati High Court.

The Mizos were the first who accepted the institution of Autonomous District Council under the provisions of the Sixth Schedule of the Constitution; and they boldly practised this new concept from 1952 to 1972. During that period, the Pawi-Lakher Regional Council was functioning with village councils at the grass-root level. In 1972, the Mizo Hills district was converted into a Union Territory. The Mizo Hills District Council was abolished as also the Pawi-Lakher Regional Council for which three new autonomous district councils, namely the Pawi Autonomous District Council, the Lakher Autonomous District Council and the Chakma Autonomous District Council were constituted.

One could say that there was stability in the Mizo Hills Autonomous District Council area from the beginning upto 1970, and elections to the District Council and the Village Councils thereunder were held at regular periodic intervals. In the newly established district councils, Pawi-Lakher and Chakma from 1972, however, there was chronic political instability. At the beginning, the contestants were all regional parties, and the national parties began to appear in the field from 1962. The political stability prevailing during 1952 to 1970 was due wholly to the Mizo Union, and it was after 1974 when they merged wholesale with the Indian National Congress, horse trading and instability began. In almost all the successive elections, the percentage of poll was always good, averaging 60 per cent and touching above 75 per cent in some constituencies. Very rarely were same members elected more than three times, - presumably a belief that no one was indispensable. While the participation of the fair sex in voting was always good, their actual participation in the contest had never been anything but poor. During 1972 to 1984, only six ladies contested the elections, and two of them were elected. Two ladies were nominated by the Central Government to the State Legislature. One lady sought election to the Lok Sabha and forfeited her security deposit. No woman had so far contested for a Rajya Sabha seat.[26]

The District and Regional Councils had wide powers and functions—legislative, executive, judicial and even financial. The legislative powers include making laws for allotment, occupation and other use of land, regulation for shifting cultivation, management and control of water courses and forests, irrigations, establishment of village councils, town committees, village police, public health and sanitation, customary laws including marriage, inheritance, divorce, money lending *et al.*

The District Council has executive powers to run and manage primary schools, dispensaries, markets, cattle ponds, ferries, village council courts, roads, bridges and a number of other welfare works, such as drinking water supply, primary health centres, specially maternity and child care and adult education.

A reference had earlier been made to the judicial set up and their function. The set up has been functioning somewhat satisfactorily. Any machinery, whether executive or judicial, to be successful, must be self-sufficient and not dependent on someone else's goodwill. The manner of raising and utilisation of funds, timely sanction of grants-in-aid from the State/Central Governments are often dependant on the goodwill of someone else and could be cause of avoidable irritations. It is not that the District Councils or the Regional Councils wherever they existed were without adequate sources of funds. Levy of tax on professions, trades and callings, tax on maintenance of schools, dispensaries, roads and ferries which the District Councils are empowered to do require expertise which is not always available in the region. Another irritant has been the share of the royalties from the extraction of minerals from the District Council areas.

It is hardly necessary to reiterate that if the District Councils were to function effectively, all help and assistance in the shape of administrative guidance and financial assistance are given timely to the Village Councils under them to take proper shape in order that they are able to discharge all their functions envisaged under the provisions of the Sixth Schedule and the rules made thereunder by the appropriate District Councils. Needless to say, failures of many of our organisations are reluctance in many cases, and inadequate delegation of powers. It had always been incomprehensible to me why we talk so much about decentralisation but never willing to grant one.

The performance of some of the District Councils might not have been wholly satisfactory in the past and some of them might have actually deserved harsh treatment after close scrutiny. Have we really examined what the causes were, and what are the remedies ? It is gratifying to note that the ambit of the Constitution (Seventy Third Amendment) Act, 1992 is not proposed to be applied to the states of Nagaland, Meghalaya and Mizoram; and the hill areas in the state of Manipur for which District Councils exist under any law for the time being in force. (Article 234M (1) (2) (a) & (b) of the above mentioned amendment of the Constitution).

After all, the autonomous District Councils in the North East have all been functioning since 1954 without any of the concerned units asking for a change. The position in respect of Arunachal Pradesh and Mizoram is slightly different from the others. The Arunachal Pradesh, previously known as North East Frontier Tract (later changed to Agency), was part of Assam included in Part B of para 20 of the Sixth Schedule of the Constitution, and was directly administered by the Governor of Assam acting as the Agent of the President of India. As such, the provisions of the Sixth Schedule of the Constitution for the autonomous district councils were not applicable to the then NEFA. This position was substantially changed, first in 1972 when NEFA was raised to the status of a Union Territory in terms of the North Eastern Areas (Reorganisation) Act, 1971 by which the name of Arunachal Pradesh was also adopted; and secondly in 1986 when it became a full-fledged state by virtue of the State of Arunachal Pradesh Act, 1986. The provisions of the Sixth Schedule are still inapplicable.

Somewhat similarly, Mizoram was raised to the status of a Union Territory by separating it from the state of Assam, again by virtue of the provisions of the North Eastern Areas (Reorganisation) Act, 1971. This was on 21 January, 1972. The Mizo District Council Courts were allowed to continue as if the areas within their jurisdiction were comprised in an autonomous district under the Sixth Schedule[27].

The birth of Bangladesh in December, 1971 altogether changed the political scenario of Mizoram. The MNF who had all along been talking in terms of secession were disillusioned and became amenable to reason to give up violence. Peace efforts which began from early 1970s but which had hardly made any headway started bearing fruits. The historic 'Peace Accord' between the Government of India and the MNF bringing to an end the 25 year long insurgency was signed and the state of Mizoram inaugurated on 20 February, 1987. This 'Peace Accord' reaffirmed the constitutional provision for the non-application of the Central Acts in Mizoram in respect of (a) social and religious practices of the Mizos; (b) Mizo customary law and procedure; (c) administration of civil and criminal justice involving decisions according to the Mizo practices and Customary laws; and (d) ownership and transfer of land, unless the Legislative Assembly of Mizoram so decided. It was also provided *inter alia* that the Inner Line Regulation would not be altered or repealed without consulting the State Government. Accordingly Article 371G was inserted in the Constitution by the Constitution (Fifty-third Amendment) Act, 1986, section 2 with effect from 20 February, 1987, the date of statehood for Mizoram. In spite of these special constitutional provisions to protect and safeguard the religious, social, customary practices and law as well as the retention of the Inner Line Regulation and the tribal land tenure system, some doubts have now crept in whether Mizoram continues to enjoy the privilege of a 'tribal area' and the status of some type analogous to those available in the autonomous district or state. This aspect of the matter should not be allowed to remain unresolved, and must be taken into consideration as and when the whole issue of whether or not the Constitution (Seventy-third Amendment) Act, 1992 is to be extended to the tribal and hill areas of the north eastern states. In this connection, mention might be made of the committee of the Chief Ministers of the seven states of the north east with Capt. W.A. Sangma, former Chief Minister of Meghalaya as the Chairman-Convenor, and Shri Lalkhama, erstwhile Chief Secretary of Mizoram, as the Secretary of the Committee. This was during the time of the late Rajiv Gandhi's Prime Ministership. This Committee was of the view that since the tribes in the seven different units of the North East are so many with diverse customs, culture, traditions, law of inheritance, ownership of land and above all such diverse customs pertaining to women, it would not be possible to consider adopting any uniform pattern such as the panchayati raj system prevailing elsewhere in the country.[28] This was indeed a very sound judgement. In this 'Foreword' to the second edition of Dr. Verrier Elwin's *A Philosophy for NEFA*, the late Prime Minister Jawaharlal Nehru wrote on 9 October, 1958 that "People should develop along the lines of their own genius and we should avoid imposing anything on them. We should try to encourage in every way their own traditional arts and culture". This was the way of discipline the officers of the frontier administration were enjoined upon to follow and is still true in today's situation.

References

1. Directorate of Economics and Statistics, Govt. of Mizoram, Aizawl, 1993.
2. Rev. Liangkhaia, *Mizo Chanchin Bul 1*, Aizawl, 1951.
3. Vumson, *Zo History*, Aizawl, Mizoram.
4. Rev. Liangkhaia, *Mizo Chanchin Bul 2*, Aizawl, Mizoram.

   K. Zawla, *Mizo Pi Pute leh an Thlahte Chanchin*, Aizawl, 1964.
5. Vumson, *Zo History*, Aizawl, Mizoram.
6. *ibid.*
7. *ibid.*
8. *ibid.*
9. R.N. Prasad, *Autonomy Movement in Mizoram*, Vikas Publishing House Pvt. Ltd., New Delhi, 1994.
10. *ibid.*
11. L.B. Thanga, *Mizo – A Study in Racial Personality*, United Publishers, Gauhati, 1978.
12. *ibid.*
13. *ibid.*
14. Zatluanga, *Mizo Chanchin*, Aizawl, 1969.
15. N.E. Parry, *Lushai Custom – A Monograph on Lushai Customs & Ceremonies*, Reprinted, Tribal Research Institute, Aizawl, Mizoram, 1988.
16. R.N. Prasad, *Autonomy Movement in Mizoram*, Vikas Publishing House Pvt. Ltd., New Delhi, 1994.
17. Quoted by R.N. Prasad, *ibid.*
18. Quoted by R.N. Prasad, *ibid.*
19. *ibid.*
20. *ibid.*
21. *ibid.*
22. *ibid.*
23. V. Venkata Rao, H. Thansang, Niru Hazarika, *A Century of Government and Politics in North East India*, Vol. 111, Mizoram, 1987.
24. *ibid.*

25. L.B. Thanga, Paper presented at Seminar on *Agrarian Structure & Land Relations in NE India* at NIRD NE-Regional Centre, Guwahati, March 22-24, 1990.

26. V. Venkata Rao, *op. cit.*

27. *ibid.*

28. *Balkhama,* Aizawl, Unpublished Document.

7

Traditional Self-Governing Institutions: A Study of Village Administration in Mizoram

– R.N. Prasad

The chieftainship originated in the physical and intellectual power of person who could established command over a large number of people and to repel any attack by other chiefs and enemies. In other words, one who had the ability to organise a force became a Chief. Such a person became the guardian and defender of his people. It, thus appears that the institution of chieftainship emerged out of the collective needs of group life which characterise tribal living. But there is no definite record when and how in the past, this institution took a concrete shape. But it can be reasonably asserted that this happened at quite an early stage of evolution in their group life.[1] The Sailos became the most powerful Chiefs and they ruled practically over the then Lushai Hills (now Mizoram) except in Pawi-Lakher region at the time of the advent of the British. Pawis and Lakhers had their own Chiefs who ruled the South-eastern part of the Lushai Hills. They had not followed the Sailo Chiefs.[2] There were Sailo and non-Sailo Chiefs. The non-Sailo Chiefs were known as *Hnamchawm* (commoners). The Sailo Chiefs were from the upper Mizo clan.

Though the Sailo Chiefs commanded more respect than others, all the Chiefs enjoyed the same powers, functions and privileges. The British rulers did not make any distinction between them. They recognised them as independent Chiefs but subject to their control. Really when the British rulers encountered them, they were rather surprised to see a large number of indigenous institutions for the administration of local or village affairs running independently of one another under the autocratic Chief of immense local standing. The institution of chieftainship was autocratic. There was a complete concentration of powers in the hands of village Chiefs and their council of elders, who used to control and regulate all aspects of the village life in accordance with the prevailing customs. Shakespeare described the Chiefs as despotic heads of small independent states. Similarly Captain T.H. Lewin, who was the first British to know the Lushais/Mizos intimately described the village system among the Mizos as a number of petty states each under a dictator or president.[3] Thus the Mizo Chiefs in the beginning opposed the British rule and so fought the British rulers with all the might at their command. But the British rulers annexed the then Lushai Hills (Mizoram) in 1890 and thereby normalised their strained relations with the main opponent - Chiefs after appeasing them with the gifts of their wise statesmanship. They divided the territory into two administrative wings, viz., The North Lushai Hills District, a part of Assam and the South Lushai Hills District, a part of Bengal. But they decided in 1898 to merge the two districts into one – the Lushai Hills District, a part of Assam under a Superintendent. The same year marked the beginning of settled administration in the district. The British made the chieftainship hereditary, because it guaranteed political stability and loyalty of the Chiefs to the Government. In 1898, a system of Land Settlement was introduced. Accordingly, each Chief was given a certain area of land to administer. The British Superintendent, thus, used the Chiefs in such way that they became the main plank of the alien rule over their own people. They laid the foundation on which the edifice of the British rule was erected. The Chiefs were made representatives of the British Government in their own land. In fact, the British Superintendent and the Chiefs ruled the people autocratically.[4]

Each Chief had territorial jurisdiction of his own, consisting of one or more villages. In fact, the Chief owned all that was in the village. Before the annexation of the Lushai Hills, the Chiefs, exercised life and death powers, though these powers and functions were not precise and definite. He was, at the same time, the supreme administrator, the Chief justice, the protector and guardian of his villagers. In running village administration, he was assisted/advised by a council of village elders called *'Upas'* in Mizo language. The elders were generally men of the Chief's chioce, nominated or selected without considering the opinion of the villagers. Most of them were either opportunists or from among the well-to-do sections of the society or royal clan. But they held office at his pleasure. The Chief was responsible for the control of the village, and had wide powers in the village administration. Besides the Upas, a number of village officials such as *Tlangau* (Village Courier/Crier, *Thirdeng* (Blacksmith), *Puithiam* (Priest), *Khawchhiar* (Village Writer), and *Remhuals* (expert jhum cultivators) were also appointed by the Chief to carry out the village administration smoothly and efficiently. The *Puithiam* was the village priest who performed all kinds of ceremonies. But with the introduction of Christianity, the position of the village priest has substantially deteriorated. However, for their important services, the village officials used to receive remuneration mostly in kind directly from the villagers. The rate of payment differed from village to village. But for all these works, the village officials were exempted from cooliwork, (*Fathang*) paddy tax and house tax. They had different duties entrusted to them by the Chief, which they were to carry out individually for the welfare of the rural masses.[5]

The Chief's and the council of elders discussed all matters of the village, asked the villagers to render voluntary services and also executed the orders and directions of the British Superintendent heading the district. The Chief also functioned as the village court to decide all types of cases, except murder and rape and disputes between the people of the village according to the Mizo customs. The cases of murder and rape were reported to the British Superintendent of the district for a trial. Since non-interference in the internal administration of the Chief was the general policy of the British Superintendent, he often upheld the decisions and acts of the Chiefs. Although the Chief was the real repository of power, yet he seldom ignored the advice of his elders and well-being of the villagers. He hardly interfered with the judgment of the elders in the trial of disputes and cases.

He thus, tried to give it the semblance of people's government in the administration of his village through the council of elders. He wielded judicial powers no doubt but he was not at all above the customary law of the land. He himself could be subjected to a group trial for exceeding the usual norms of the Mizo society. But the political system was such that no one could dare to speak against his activities or to criticise any act of his. The authority of the Chief was also safeguarded by the Superintendent. Besides, the villagers were also bound by the traditional custom to obey him implicitly and also carry out his order without any condition. Theoretically, the Chief was all powerful and a despotic ruler. But the social mores were so shaped through the process of evolution that he could seldom afford to exercise unrestricted powers over his people. In fact, his rule could not be malevolent as the villagers could always migrate to another village in the jurisdiction of some other Chief.[6]

The Pawis and Lakhers in the South Lushai Hills (Mizoram) had their own Chiefs. The chieftainship among the Pawis was the same as among the Mizos. The Lakher chieftainship was, however, a little different. Shakespeare found the Lakhers in common with the Chins as being less democratic than the Lushais. The power of the Chiefs was greater and the Chiefs' relatives and other wealthy people found a kind of peerage. The Lakhers had no single royal clan like the Sailo clan among the Mizos. Each Lakher tribe had its own royal clan. The Chief had full power over the villagers. He could impose fines and in the extreme case, turn a villager out of the village. The Lakher chieftainship was hereditary, the eldest son succeeding the father.[7]

The Chief, as a token of respect for his being head of the village administration, was entitled to certain privileges from the villagers such as a flesh tax (*Sachhiah*), a paddy tax (*Fathang*), salt tax (*Chichhiah*) and meat tax (*Sachhiah*) etc. He could also seize any villager's property who failed to carry out his judicial orders. He had the privilege to keep the slaves (*Bawis*) as well as to get his house constructed and repaired with the free labour of the villagers. Here it is true that the Chief and his counsellors formed the royal or upper class of the Mizo village society. The Chiefs sometimes abused and misused their rights and privileges by treating the villagers as their personal servants. It is surprising to note that even in cases of misuse of powers and privileges by the Chief, the Superintendent never interfered. He always upheld such steps of the Chiefs and protected them fully to retain the colonial regime in the area. So the villagers felt that the Chief's rule was oppressive and unbearable. They also felt exploited at the Chief's hands.

This position, however, changed later on and the British Superintendent curtailed such traditional powers of the Chief as inflicting capital punishment, seizing food stores and property of villagers, grabbing their lands, taxing traders, appointing his son as Chief and judicial supremacy/ powers. Thus the Chief practically lost their rights and privileges to the British masters. However, while the powers of the Chiefs in relation to the British masters declined, his powers over the people, however, increased further. This was partly due to the policy of non-interference of the British rulers in the internal affairs of the tribesmen. Thus apparently, the main motive behind curtailment of the Chiefs' traditional rights by the British Superintendent was to have more control over the turbulent people and also of the Chiefs. The Superintendent used the Chiefs as agents of the British imperialist rule in Mizoram with practically no expenditure. The Chief acted as a link between the villagers and the Superintendent. In fact, the Chiefs became the local representatives of the alien government after the people giving up their migratory habit. To achieve this objective, the British allowed the indigenous institution of the chieftainship to continue, though gradually there was an erosion in the powers and privileges of the Chiefs.

This exploitative institution of the chieftainship continued even in the post-independent India for some years. But this political enslavement of the Mizo people at the hands of the Superintendent and the Chiefs brought about political consciousness, awakening and other qualitative changes among the educated Mizo youth, who became totally opposed to the Chiefs and elders for continuing the imperialist rule in Mizoram.

After India achieved independence, a new scheme of administration for the hills districts of Assam based on the recommendations of the North-East Frontier Tribal and Excluded Areas Sub-Committee of the Constituent Assembly, known as the Bardoloi Committee was incorporated in the Part 'A' of the Sixth Schedule to the Constitution of India. As a result, the Mizo District Council for the Mizos and the Pawi-Lakher Regional Council for Pawi, Lakher and Chakma tribes were set up in 1952 and 1953 respectively. With the introduction of the District Council, the high powered post of Superintendent was abolished and the whole area was put under a Deputy Commissioner with much curtailed powers, and the Chief Executive Members of the District and Regional Councils. The District and the Regional Council, a democratic autonomous political institution created under the Sixth Schedule of the Indian Constitution also threatened the position and privileges of the Chiefs, because as per the provision under para 3 of the Sixth Schedule, the District Council can regulate the succession, appointment and even abolition of the institution of village Chiefs and headman. As a result the Chiefs became no more than village headmen under the Mizo District Council. In the first elections to the District Council, the Mizo Union, which had a clear economic programme of fighting the vested interests of the Chiefs, made a significant dent in the rural segments and also captured powers in the District Council. Holding the reigns of the District Council administration, the Mizo Union enacted the Lushai Hills District (Social Custom and Practices) Act in May 1953 and abolished the special privileges or traditional dues of the Chiefs and their elders. Similarly, the Pawi-Lakher Regional Council enacted the Pawi-Lakher Autonomous Region (Social Customs and Practices) Act in December 1953 and also abolished the traditional dues payable to the Chiefs within the jurisdiction. Further, the Mizo District Council persuaded the Government of Assam to abolish the chieftainship. Accordingly, the Government enacted the Assam Lushai Hills District (Acquisition of Chief's Rights) Act 1954 and abolished the autocratic hereditary chieftainship in the area covered by the Mizo District Council. Under the same Act, the chiefship within the jurisdiction of the Pawi-Lakher Regional Council was also abolished. The Chiefs were compensated in cash for the loss of their tributes and powers. The abolition of the chiefship was fully justified in keeping with the fulfilment of the democratic aspirations of the common Mizos, the democratic provisions of the Sixth Schedule to the Constitution of India and also the economic programme of fighting the vested interests of the Chiefs as alleged by the Mizo

Union. So the abolition of chiefship became an expedient and as a result, it was done away with. This step was appreciated by the Mizo commoners. The abolition of chieftainship has definitely provided opportunities to a large number of the Mizos to participate in decision making.

Village Council

After the District and the Regional Councils democratised the village administration by enacting the Lushai Hills District (Village Councils) Act in December 1953 and the Pawi-Lukher Regional (Village Councils) Act in September 1954, the village administration in Mizoram was vested in the democratically constituted Village Councils, which in fact started functioning from 1954 and 1955 under the respective jurisdictions of the Councils. But when Mizoram attained the status of a Union Territory and later that of a State, the Government of Mizoram adopted the Lushai Hills District (Village Councils) Act 1953 for the administration of the village affairs in the areas specified by the Act which was also amended in 1991. The administration of the Village Councils was put under the Department of Local Administration, Town Planning and Housing. But in the new administrative set-up, the Pawi-Lakher Regional Council was bifurcated into three viz.: The Mara Autonomous District Council, the Lai Autonomous District Council and the Chakma Autonomous District Council. These Councils have also adapted the Pawi-Lakher Autonomous Regional (Village Councils) Act in their respective jurisdictions. So the Mara District Council, the Lai District Council and the Chakma District Council manage village affairs in their jurisdictions through Village Councils over which the Government of Mizoram has no control. Briefly, Mizoram has now two sets of the Village Councils over which the Government of Mizoram and the District Councils extend their jurisdiction independently.[8]

Composition of Village Councils

According to the Village Council Act, there is a Village Council for each village. Each Village Council consists of 4 to 15 members according to the number of house as specified by the Act. Of these, one-fourth are nominated by the Government of Mizoram and the Executive Committee of the Mara Autonomous District Council, the Lai Autonomous District Council and the Chakma Autonomous District Council respectively and the rest elected according to the provisions of the Village Council Election Rules on the basis of adult franchise, mostly by secret ballot for a period of three years. Though the number of members of the Village Councils may vary from village to village, the term of a Village Council may be extended or reduced by the orders of the Government and the District Councils. If the Village Council is unable to carry on the village administration efficiently, the District Council can dissolve such Village Council and during the period of dissolution, the Circle Assistant or some other officers of the Council may be appointed to look after the administration of the dissolved Village Council. It is also mentioned in the Act that a member, who is nominated to a Village Council, may hold office during the pleasure of the government and the Executive Committees of the Councils. If a member absents himself continuously in ten consecutive meetings of a Village Council without prior permission, the Village Council may in a meeting specially convened for the purpose, declare his seat vacant after giving him an opportunity for a hearing and in such case, the Village Council communicates the decision to the government and the Executive Committees.

For elections, there is an electoral roll and polling station for each village constituency. For each constituency, a returning officer is appointed to receive and scrutinize nomination papers of the candidates and to fix the date and time for polling. He also acts as the presiding officer on the election day, and after the poll is over, he counts votes and declares results on the same day. Each candidate is also allotted an election symbol and a ballot box. Each voter is given ballot papers according to the number of seats to be filled up through election. Besides, all other Village Council election rules are observed.[9]

Village Council Executive

Each Village Council has the Executive Committee consisting of President, Vice-President and a Secretary. The President and Vice-President are elected by the members of the Village Council from among themselves. The Secretary is appointed by the Government/the District Councils on the advice of President, who is in any case not a member of the Village Council. The executive functions of the Village Council are thus vested in three persons. The President presides over all the meetings of the Village Council. He also summons the meetings whenever necessity arises. All proposals and questions are decided in the meetings by a majority of votes. The President preserves order and exercises all powers necessary to enforce the decisions taken in the meetings. If a member fails to carry out the direction of the President, he reports this in writing to the Government/Executive Committees of the Councils. On receipt of such report, the Government/Executive Committees may, if it deems necessary, suspend the member for any period.[10]

Besides, it is also the President's responsibility to issue notice/instruction for prevention of dangers, such as outbreak of fire, epidemic etc. in the village. He carries out all orders/notifications issued either by the Deputy Commissioner or the District Councils. He also acts as the Treasurer of the Village Council Fund into which collections made by the Village Council are deposited. The list of collection is maintained by the Secretary and any subscriber can check the accounts. The President examines the registers/books kept by the Secretary. The Vice-President, in the absence of the President, performs all official duties of the President.[11]

Let us now examine the position of the Secretary in the Village Council's administration. The Secretary is the village writer and records all proceedings of the Village Council and the Village Council court which are signed by the President. If necessary, he publishes all orders and proceedings duly signed by the President. He also keeps all the books and records of the Council and of the village court, which can be examined by the officers of the District Councils or any member of the Village Council appointed on this behalf. The Secretary holds office as long as the Village Council executive considers his work and conduct fit and satisfactory.[12]

It may be added here that the President is the Chief non-official functionary at the village level and the village Secretary is the main official functionary and administrative assistant to the village executive. He, thus, acts as the agent of executive committee and the Government. He reports about the poor harvest to the government for remedial measure, severe incident (if any) and the villager's needs such as opening of school and post office.

Functions of Village Council

The functions of the Village Council are classified into two categories: administrative and judicial.

Administrative

The administrative functions of the Village Council include construction and maintenance of inter-village paths, roads, maintenance of water supply points and their approach roads, distribution of jhum plots by draws of lots, construction and maintenance of approach foot paths to jhum, allotment of house sites in the village, maintenance of register for birth and deaths, maintenance of burial grounds, regulation of *Hntlang* i.e. voluntary services for community work and preservation and maintenance of village safety and collection of taxes.

A mention with regard to *Hnatlang, Jhumlands* and house sites may be made to explain the administration of these duties. The Village Council can enforce *Hnatlang* in the interest of the villagers on any persons irrespective of religion, caste or class whenever occasion so demands. The order also extends to a Government servant. Any person, who does not comply with the order of *Hnatlang* is liable to pay fine in kind or cash : the Village Council can exempt any person of the age of 60 years or above or those below 15 years of age.

With regard to jhumlands, if there is a dispute in the allotment of jhum plots, the Governor or any other officer authorized by him can intervene; in case of the Village Councils under the District Councils, the Executive Committees intervene.

As regards the house sites, the Village Council can evict a person having unauthorised occupation of land and can also order for vacation within seven days. However, if the erring person persists beyond that limit, the Village Council can order for demolition of the building or any structure on the unauthorised land or impose fine so long as the unauthorised occupant persists.

Besides, the Village Council forms the Sanitation Committee with a view to carrying out sanitation works and cleanliness in the village. It also takes necessary step to prevent and control fire and epidemic in the village. It can also pass orders under *Mizo Hnam Dan* (customary law) to run the village administration smoothly. The Council also appoints *Tlangau,* the village courier / crier in each village to bring all the orders, notifications of the Council and government to the villagers, carry summons of the Village Council court to all parties and other persons to attend the court meeting as also the President's notice to all members of the council to attend all meetings. For this service, he is exempted from *Hnatlang*. If in any village, no *Tlangau* is found on the remuneration granted under the sub-section of the Act, the Executive Committee may by order raise additional remunerations from the villagers to be paid either in cash or in kind, the amount of which to be fixed in consultation with the Village Council concerned. Thus we see that of the administration duties, some are provided for in the Act, Rules and Regulations, while others are based on convention, usage, practice and custom of the Mizo people.[13]

Judicial

A Village Council court has been provided for each village in the rules, constituted under the Administration of Justice Rules, 1953. The court comprises three members, selected by the council from among its elected members, with a three-year term of office. It actually resembles *Gram Katchery*, a judicial organ of the *Gram Panchayat* of the plains districts, where administration of justice is vested with the democratically elected members. When the Council sits as a court, three members are required to constitute the quorum. The Village Council court is the lowest court under the District Councils. The Village Council Courts of Aizawl and Lunglei districts are under the Government of Mizoram. The Village Council court tries suits and cases of civil and miscellaneous nature between the tribals in the village in accordance with the customary laws of the land. It also tries criminal cases falling within the customary laws and offences of petty nature, such as petty theft and pilferage, mischief and trespass of petty nature, simple assault and hurt, affront and affray of whatever kind, drunken or disorderly brawling, public nuisance etc. The Village Council can impose a fine for any of these offence and can order any accused or witness to appear before the court for examination. If such person fails to appear, the Village Council is competent to impose a fine.

The Village Council has no power to try offences for which imprisonment is obligatory under the Indian Panel Code. It is also not competent to try cases of heinous crimes like murder, rape, sexual intercourse with minor girl and sodomy, nor can it decide inheritance cases which is within the purview of the customary law.

An appeal against any order, sentence, decision of the Village Council court lies with the Subordinate District Council Court or Additional Subordinate District Council Court within 60 days of the conviction or decision. No legal practitioner is allowed to appear before a Village Council court bench. In a nutshell, the organisation of village judiciary is a step in the direction of the decentralization of administration of justice.[14]

Village Council in Practice

Let us now examine some of the major problems confronting the operation of the Village Councils in Mizoram. It is observed that the Village Council is suffering from a number of weaknesses. The District Council is empowered to make laws regarding the establishment of Village Council to carry on the day to day administration of village but no effort has been made either in the initial stages or even later after gaining experience to make it effective. The administrative limitation's mainly relate to inadequacy of trained personnel, heavy load of works of multifarious nature, mostly administrative and non-developmental. It is necessary to train them, if they have to make Village Council successful. The Village Council set up by the District Councils and the Government of Mizoram are administrative and judiciary bodies and solving socio-economic problems of the villagers is beyond its scope. Non-involvement of the Village Council in developmental schemes, programmes, planning process at micro level and execution, therefore, seems to be one of the biggest mistakes. So in the Act, suitable amendment should be made to involve the Village Councils in development activities, planning process and implementation of programmes. The Village Council has financial limitations due to paucity of funds. According to the provisions of the Act, the Village Council is also custodian of 'Village Council Fund' or finance. The word 'finance' suggests money., but there is no monetary fund in the village. No permanent source of income is mentioned in the Act except imposition of fine on the accused or on those who absent themselves from '*Hnatlang*'. These are purely deterrent in nature and hence insignificant as revenue sources. '*Fathang*' (Paddy Tax), another source of income with the Village Council does no longer exist in the fast changing society of the Mizos. Thus the Village Councils are very weak financially, having no funds at their disposal to carry out their own programmes. So they have remained 'empty boxes' without much stuff in them. Attempts should be made to mobilize financial resources for Village Councils to enable them to function as an effective institution of grass roots democracy for development, welfare, justice and dignity of man.[15]

It is surprising to note that the Village Council, being the supreme unit of self-government at the grass roots level, lacks power in important matters as taxation and tax collection (land revenue). These taxes are collected by the Department of Land Revenue and Settlement, Government of Mizoram and the District Councils in their respective jurisdictions, though the existing Act empowers the Village Councils to collect such taxes. Measures should be taken to restore such powers of the councils to make them fund raising institutions for village development plans. It is also suggested that from the budgets of both the state government and the District Councils, fifty per cent of the funds allocated for development activities should be transferred to the Village Councils.

The Councils have failed to evoke the local initiative and people's participation in the developmental activities as well as to bring about social and economic changes in the tribal areas to the desired extent mainly owing to a strong tendency towards centralisation in the state, though there is a talk of decentralisation of power to district and lower level bodies. Such a process of centralisation is just not compatible with the talk of decentralisation of planning. Besides, there is less and less willingness on the part of the State Government and the District Councils to share power with lower elected bodies. As a result, the Village Councils are not getting economic or political power. As long as this trend continues, the Village Councils will not play a vital role in the socio-economic transformation of the rural tribesmen. So it is suggested that the Village Councils should be given an adequate devolution of financial resources, powers and responsibilities.

Not only that, available information indicates that perhaps many Village Councils have not yet been provided with office accommodation by the government and the District Councils. As such, the Village Council executives and members have no place to sit together, convene meeting, drawing up plans and schemes for development ad reconstruction, preserve records of meetings, and documents concerned with the village administration. The result has been that the councils have not been functioning effectively and securing public participation and co-operation in rural administration. It is, therefore, felt necessary that the government and the District Councils on their own initiative should help construction of the council's offices to ensure efficacy in the functioning of the village government.

Surprisingly, the Government of Mizoram has declared Aizawl, Lunglei, Saiha, Champhai, Serchhip and Kolasib as urban areas but has not so far provided for the pattern of urban administration. Instead, the Village Councils meant for the village administration, are still allowed to continue functioning in the urban areas of Mizoram with much curtailed powers. For instance, the Village Council is empowered to allot house sites in both the rural and urban areas but this power of allotting house sites in the urban areas has been curtailed and vested with the government. It is, thus, obvious that the Village Councils existing in the urban areas of Mizoram have completely become redundant institutions. No where in the country, such practice of making rural administrative institutions to function in the urban areas is found. Thus, the functions of urban administration have been entrusted mostly to the Deputy Commissioner, head official functionary of the district, and the Village Council President, a chief non-official functionary of the district at the village level. This has caused a lot of confusions which are likely to create many problems in the field of local self government as also urban government in the long run. Since the process of urbanisation is on, the government and the District Councils must consider substitution of the Village Council by same pattern of municipal administration for urban areas which are outgrowing the characteristics of the village. Here it may be suggested that the government should consider adoption of the constitutional provisions relating to municipalities (The Constitution seventy fourth amendment) Act, 1992 and enact legislation keeping in view of the local situations. This will certainly help encouraging participatory decision making at micro level by involving urban people and people's representatives in decision making process in various areas of activities which fall in the purview of the lower level micro-level units.

The Village Council should also work for sensitising people, specially the poor, and make them aware about their plight, their rights and their role in rural development.

Thus, it may be concluded that Village Councils have neither created a significant impact at the village level nor have provided effective leadership to local community due to lack of financial resources and devolution of powers and responsibilities.

If the Village Council, a grassroots institution of democracy constituted under the provisions of the Sixth Schedule to the Constitution of India has to function effectively, the Act should be suitably amended to strengthen it structurally and operationally, providing greater autonomy to the Council in administrative, political, financial, judicial and developmental spheres/domains and also transform it into an effective unit for formulation and executing the plans of economic development and rural reconstruction on the pattern of other democratically elected village institutions like panchayats.

Mizoram and the Constitution (Seventy-third Amendment) Act, 1992

With a view to improving the participation of the rural people in the process of their development and also the involvement of people in the process of decision making directly affecting their life, the Government of India has provided a constitutional status for the village panchayats under the Constitution (seventy third amendment) Act, 1992 which was ratified by legislatures of more than half the states including the state of Mizoram. After ractification, the President assented this bill on April 20, 1993 which later became an Act. This Act was brought into force by a notification with effect from April 24, 1993. Accordingly, the provisions of the Constitution Amendment Act are incorporated in the Acts of the states and institutions are established at different levels in order to improve the quality of implementation of programmes. The State governments were to devolve adequate functions, finances and powers to ensure better implementation of various developmental programmes. Not only this but the formation of Panchayats in some hills areas as per the provisions of the constitution (seventy third amendment) Act, 1992 has become mandatory and constitutional obligation for the state government.

However, some of the north-eastern states like Nagaland, Meghalaya and Mizoram have been kept outside the purview of the constitutional provisions relating to panchayats under the 73rd amendment to the Constitution, though the legislature of these states have already approved the Act but also denied the application of the constitutional provisions relating to panchayats to their respective states on the ground that traditional self governing institutions to carry on the village administration have already been in operation in these states since pre and post independent India. For instance, the Government of Mizoram and the Mara District Council, the Lai District Council and the Chakma District Council have refused the application of constitutional provisions concerning Panchayati Raj systems mainly owing to the operation of democratically elected Village Councils in their respective jurisdiction since 1954 and 1955 respectively which have been set up under sub-clause (ii) of clause (3) of the Sixth Schedule to the Constitution of India and accordingly, the Village Council has been given a constitutional status with a very limited functions/powers, mostly administrative and judicial of petty nature under the Lushai Hills District (Village Council) Act, 1953 and the Pawi-Lakher Autonomous Region (Village Council) Act, 1954. These Acts have been adopted by the Government of Mizoram and the District Councils since 1972. But it appears from the analysis of the Village Council Acts that the Councils have been denied the devolution of financial resources and political powers and responsibilities. Briefly, the Councils lack of political decentralisation and economic decentralisation whereas the panchayat system under the 73rd amendment to the Constitution has to play three important roles in the country such as decentralisation of administrative, financial and political powers, contribution towards strengthening the planning process at the micro level and overall rural development and improvement of the access of the poor rural masses to decision making bodies. These roles have already been incorporated in the Eleventh Schedule (Article 243-G) of the Constitution (seventy third amendment) Act, 1992, which are classified into twenty nine functions/ powers of socio-cultural and econo-political nature.[17] Thus both the Village Councils and Panchayati Raj institutions are the creation of the Constitution of India, no doubt, but they differ structurally and operationally. But Panchayati Raj institutions have larger scopes to deliver the goods for the greatest number in the rural society whereas the socio-cultural and econo-political transformation of the poor tribesmen is beyond the scope of the Village Councils. Therefore, the application of constitutional provisions relating to panchayats by the government and the District Councils to their respective jurisdiction is an imperative need.

References

1. R.N. Prasad, *'Traditional Political Institution of Chieftainship in Mizoram; Powers, Functions, Position and Privileges,* Paper presented at International Seminar on Studies on the Minority Nationalities of North East India - The Mizos, organised by Directorate of Higher and Technical Education, Government of Mizoram, Aizwal on April, 7-9, 1992 and published in the form of Seminar paper, p. 50.

2. *ibid*, p. 50.

3. *ibid*, p. 50.

4. *ibid*, p. 50.

5. *ibid*, p. 51.

6. R.N. Prasad and A.K. Agarwal (ed.) *Political and Economic Development of Mizoram,* New Delhi, Mittal Publications, 1991, p. 114.

7. R.N. Prasad, *op. cit.* P. 52.

8. R. N. Prasad and A.K. Agarwal, *op. cit.*, pp. 115-117.

9. *ibid*, p. 117.

10. *ibid*, pp. 117-18.

11. *ibid*, p. 118.

12. *ibid*, p. 118.
13. *ibid*, pp. 119-20.
14. *ibid*, pp. 120-21.
15. *ibid*, p. 121.
16. *ibid*, p. 122.
17. Constitutional Provisions Relating to Village Panchayats and Municipalities in India containing Text of the Constitution (Seventy Third Amendment, Act) 1992 and the Constitution (Seventy Fourth Amendment) Act, 1992, Eastern Book Company, 34 Lalbagh, Lucknow, 1993. p. 8.

8

Traditional Self-Governing Institutions Among the Tribes of Arunachal Pradesh

– *A.C. Talukdar*

Introduction

The term 'traditional self governing institution' is used in this paper to denote the age-old socio-political institutions prevalent among the tribes of Arunachal Pradesh, maintaining order in the society, settling disputes and administering the village. In this sense the tribes of Arunachal Pradesh have a long tradition of self-governing institutions. The traditional Village Councils prevalent among them functioned as effective village governments in the past. During the British period they played an important role in the politico-administrative system of the area and received considerable encouragement for their functioning and further development from the colonial rulers as they were reluctant to extend their administration beyond a few administrative centres. After independence, the NEFA administration continued the same policy for more than two decades till the introduction of the statutory panchayats in 1969. Even today the traditional Village Council system continues to function in every tribal village.

The aim of this paper is to make a brief study of the traditional self-governing institutions prevalent among the different tribes of Arunachal Pradesh and to try to evaluate their position in village administration. An attempt is also made to examine the trend of change in them, if any. The study is based on author's own observation of the functioning of these institutions among certain tribes and his interview with a good number of traditional leaders and educated youths belonging to these tribes. Works of the State Research Department as well as works of other scholars published and unpublished are also used as source materials.

With 26 major tribes[1] and more than 100 sub-tribes, Arunachal Pradesh is a fascinatingly heterogeneous tribal state. Since each tribe and even a sub-tribe speaks its own dialect, there is no common language for the whole state. A simplified version of Assamese is generally used, in most part, for inter tribal communication and the educated Arunachalis are increasingly using Hindi and English as their lingua-franca. Unlike in the other North Eastern States the role of Christian missionaries in education and medical care is negligible here although of late a sizable number of people belonging to certain tribes have embraced Christianity.

The economy of the state is mainly agrarian and although in decline, jhuming (shifting cultivation) is still in vogue among all the tribes. In recent years, due to a variety of governmental measures and developmental activities, a section of the population among certain tribes has taken to settled cultivation in addition to jhuming. According to tradition, land belongs to the whole village among certain tribes. Each family in the village is allotted a plot of cultivable land which is treated as a private holding as long as the plot is under cultivation. The forest and fallow lands are commonly held and are used by the whole community. There are however certain variations from tribe to tribe in land holding pattern and most of the newly reclaimed 'wet rice cultivation' plots have become private holdings.

With a total area of 83,743 square kilometres, Arunachal Pradesh is the largest state among the states of North Eastern

Region of India. But most of the areas are steep hills and difficult terrains. A large number of fast flowing rivers and rivulets crisscross the area at frequent intervals. Population density in the state is thin and literacy rate low. 12.80 per cent of the population live in urban administrative centres where a large section of the population is non-tribal coming from other parts of the country mostly as government service holders and traders.

The geographical compulsion and socio-economic backwardness of the area make transport and communications very difficult even today which compelled the different tribal groups to confine themselves to a particular area and to develop a strong isolationist tendency in the past. Moreover, the traditional animosities among different tribes and an incredibly simple and primitive economy kept the inter-tribal and even inter-village interaction at the minimal level for a long time. The various tribes living in the state therefore evolved their own system of self-governing institutions for maintaining their social order and for delivering justice.

The Village Councils

Although common descent, kinship, and blood relations generally form the basis of political union among the tribal people, territorial compactness appears to be the dominating factor of political union among the tribes of Arunachal Pradesh[2]. This is evident from the fact that even where there is a tribal level organisation, Village Councils form the basic units of such organisation, or when a new village is formed out of the migrated people of a former village they form a new Village Council for themselves independent of their parent village. Similarly neighbouring villages of the same tribe have their own Village Councils although they may sometimes have an inter-village council too. Almost all the traditional institutions found among the tribes of Arunachal Pradesh are thus village level institutions and are referred to as Village Councils.

There are almost as many types of Village Councils as there are tribes in the state. The most prominent among them are the *Kebang* of the Adis, *Buliang* of the Apatanis, the *Byele* of the Nishings, the *Mele* of the Hrussos, the *Tsorgen* of the Monpas, the *Jung* of the Cherdukpens, the *Abbala* of the Idu Mishmis, the *Pharai* of the Kaman Mishmiss the *Mockchup* of the Khamtis, the *Ngothun* of the Noctes, *Wangsa-Wangsu* or *Ngopho* of the Wanchos[3] and the *Mungphong* or *Nockthung* of the Tangsas[4]. They however do not present a uniform pattern of political institution. Some of them are republics others are monarchical, some are democracies of direct type, others function through a small representative body. A few are oligarchies in nature limiting the choice of membership of the council to certain houses or clans. The *Kebang* of the Adis is a sort of direct democracy while the *Mele* of the Hrunos or the Monpa *Tsorgen* is a representative democracy. The Sherdukpen Jung or the *Apatani Buliang* on the other hand provide a clan oligarchic model. The Village Council systems found among the Khamtis, Noctes; Wanchos, Singhos and the Tangsas can be called chieftaincies. However even the oligarchic or the monarchical systems too have some elements of democracy in them while all the systems have a gerentocratic tendency in their constitution. The Monpa *Mangjomsa/Tsorgen* system has a theocratic character too as the elected head (the *Tsorgen*) also acts as the religious head in the village.

We briefly discuss below some representative systems of the different type.

The Kebang System

The *Kebang* of the Adi group of tribes[5] is the best example of a democratic set up of traditional Village Councils of Arunachal Pradesh. It is the most developed among the traditional self-governing institutions of the tribes of Arunachal Pradesh and it has acquired certain degree of sophistication and formalities in its functioning. Every Adi village has a *Kebang* of its own and it functions as a direct democracy.

The Ramos and Pailibos, the two neighbouring tribes of the Adis have a slightly variant form where *'Gembus'* (leading man of the village) play a leading role in convening and functioning of a sort of adhoc *Kebang*[6]. It is normally concerned with the administration of justice only. This is also the case with the *'Nyele'* of the Nishings where the *Gindung* plays a dominant role in convening its session and conducting its proceedings. Incidentally the *Nyele* is a very informal type of Village Council and its sessions are very infrequent and occasional. This is the reason why many scholars failed to notice this institution[6].

The *Kebang* is composed of all adult male members of the village who automatically become its member. The test of adulthood is based not on age but on physical, mental and sexual abilities. However an adult male may be temporarily debarred from attending *Kebang* under certain taboos. Women normally do not take part in the proceedings of the *Kebang* except for giving evidence or lodging a complaint.

There is no presiding officer of the *Kebang*. Discussions are formally opened by one of the experienced and elderly persons with an *'Abe'* (introductory speech) which eulogises the great role of the *Kebang* and calls upon the members to live up to its great tradition. Normally, senior members present are given precedence in speaking, and those who have acquired recognition for their oratory, wisdom and knowledge and customary laws are spontaneously allowed to lead the deliberations. The juniors in age and status, observe deference to the seniors. Capable young men with an ambition for leadership never miss an opportunity to address the *Kebang*, soon after the elders have spoken. Every member present, however, is counted as equal and has the freedom to express his ideas, views and opinion on the issue discussed. All matters that come before the *Kebang* are discussed, debated and argued in a threadbare manner. Decisions are taken by arriving at a consensus, if necessary after a very prolonged discussion. Once a decision is arrived at it is announced by one of the leading members of the *Kebang* and it is binding on all members of the village. Thus an air of spontaneity pervades the whole proceedings of a *Kebang*.

The most important and the most elaborate function of the *Kebang* is, of course, the administration of justice in the village. But it concerns itself with all other activities in the village. It looks after the day-to-day administration of the village. It watches over the welfare and well being of the village community. The opening of a new agricultural plot, building of new houses, settling of newcomers, selection of site for a school/health centre are all decided by the *Kebang*. As Varrier Elwin observes, it decides where and when to clear the jungles for cultivation, where and in what manner the festivals and the taboos are to be observed, where and when to conduct the community hunting and fishing etc. It receives important visitors to the village. It extends relief and help to persons in distress. It also receives the government circulars and notices and informs the villagers of the contents[7]. Thus the *Kebang*'s function includes administrative, developmental and judicial activities in the village making it a real village government. It also has its political activities. It settles inter-village problems and disputes through the *Bango Kebang* which consists of the representatives of several villages and sends its representatives to tribe assemblies known as the *Bogum Bokang Kebang*.

The *Kebang* still continues to perform these functions although may be in lesser degree due to the introduction of the statutory panchayats and their linkage with the higher level set ups.

The leadership of the *Kebang* is a collective one and no individual member is allowed to shoulder the responsibility of leadership alone. Theoretically no power of the *Kebang* can be enjoyed by its leaders. It always rests with the whole *Kebang*. However in reality, the Gaonburha of the village (official village headman) because of his links with the government enjoys an elevated position. Also a hierarchy of members grow in importance, in every village because of their status and capability. This hierarchy is more pronounced among the Gallos than among the Miniyongs and Padams. They however do not enjoy any official position in the *Kebang*. They only indicate their personal status and prestige enjoyed in public estimate because of their talent, endeavour and achievements. Such recognitions are gained through age, knowledge of customary laws and years of experience and proven ability.

In recent years however the *Kebang* system has undergone certain changes under the influence of the statutory panchayats working in the villages. The elected members of the panchayats are emerging as influential members of the *Kebang*. The author found that in many villages in East Siang district the Anchal Samiti panchayat members tend to dominate the proceedings of the *Kebang*. Due to their linkage with higher level politicians, they command respect from the villagers in spite of their comparative young age and lack of knowledge of customary laws. This has given birth to a set of instant leadership in the *Kebang*. The decision-making process is also undergoing certain changes. In place of the consensus process, gradually an element of forcing a decision by majority is creeping into it. Another important change noticed is in its functions[8]. The *Kebang* gradually appears to be withdrawing itself from its developmental functions except deciding the developmental requirement of the village. It is observed that many East Siang villages where formerly the developmental activities of the village such as building a schools house, constructing a path or a link road or digging a water channel used to be decided and carried out by the *Kebang* out of its own resources, now-a-days they are expected to be done out of governmental resources through the panchayats.

The Tsorgen System

Like the *Kebang* of the Adis the *Tsorgen* system of the Northern Monpas is also a well developed self-governing institution. Although a traditional tribal institution, it compares well with any modern governmental system. There is some variation of the system between the northern and the southern Monpas where it is commonly known as the *Mangjomsa* (assembly of the people). The composition of the system is more or less the same among all the Monpas, but it is more elaborate and formal among the northern Monpas. Besides, this is the only council where the members and the Head of the Council (the *Tsorgen*) are elected at least in theory for a definite term.

The *Tsorgen* system consists of the *Tso-Tsangzan* (the village assembly), the *Tsoblas* (the representative of the different segments of the village), the *Thumis* (assistants to *Tsoblas*) and the *Gumins* (the messenger) and the council of elders.[9]

The *Tso-Singjom* (village assembly) consists of all the *Khreimins* (those who contribute to the village fund). It is the General Assembly of the village and hence the highest authority in the village. However, it meets only occasionally to hear the complaints against a *Tsorgen* or to elect him. Of course, in certain villages it meets at least once a year. It does not concern itself with normal administration of the village which task is solely entrusted to the Council and the *Tsorgen*.

The Council consists of the *Tsoblas* (representatives of the village segments or hamlets constituting a village), the *Thumis* (assistant to *Tsoblas*) and the *Gumin* (the messenger). The

Tsoblas, and the *Thumis* are elected or chosen by each hamlet or a village segment. The *Gumins* are generally chosen for one year. In their respective hamlets the *Tsoblas* perform the task of the *Tsorgen*. The *Thumis* and the *Gumins* help the *Tsoblas* as well as the *Tsorgen* in discharging their functions as and when it is necessary.

The most important position in the whole system is occupied by the *Tsorgen*. He is the Chief executive authority in the village or a group of villages under him. The only authority above him is the *Tso-Tsangjom* or the General Assembly of the village. A *Tsorgen* is elected by the heads of the whole village in the General Assembly of the village. As and when the office of *Tsorgenship* falls vacant, the *Tsoblas* of the village prepare a panel of few eligible persons. The voters are then given a ballot normally 3 days ahead of the election day. Voting in the election of a *Tsorgen* is compulsory. A *Tsorgen* is normally elected for three years . But in practice once a *Tsorgen* is elected he is re-elected again and again till his death or till he becomes incapable of discharging his duties due to old age or other reasons. Occasion for preparation of a panel is also very rare. The *Tsoblas* generally agree upon a single person as the most suitable candidate and then they go to him for obtaining his consent. Once he agrees, his name is put before the General Assembly for formal election.

The *Tsorgen* is the Chief administrator of the village. He is also competent to decide all civil and criminal cases. He is expected to guide and advise the village in all matters concerning the village or a household. He is to supervise the organisation and performance of all religious ceremonies in the village. He oversees the routine administration of the village, and plays a vital role in its developmental activities. In all these activities the *Tsorgen* may take the help of the Council, the *Thumis* and the *Gumins*. He may entrust some of his works to the *Tsoblas* concerning their areas. But a Tsobla cannot decide a case on his own, he has is to do so with the help of the *Mangma* (panel of villagers or jurors) of his hamlet.

The *Tsorgen* system is so developed that it has a system of paying formal salary to the *Tsorgen*. Every house-holder in the village is required to pay *Blankpas* to the *Tsorgen* as his salary. The *Blankpa* is equivalent to one man's labour for one day and may be paid in cash or kind. Besides in certain villages there is a system of paying some tax to the *Tsorgen*. But the amount cannot be utilised by the *Tsorgen* for personal purposes, and he is to maintain proper account for it.

The *Tsorgen* system of the Northern Monpas is an institution of great effectiveness and vitality. it is as good and as well organised as any modern governmental set up. The introduction of panchayats because of its statutory status and link with the higher level government have naturally affected the authority and status of the *Tsorgen* system to some extent. But due to its theocratic and gerentocratic nature, its authority and influence have not yet eroded to any considerable extent and it continues to enjoy more or less the same status as an institution of village self government as it did in the past.

The Buliang System

The Apatani *Buliang* or Sherdukpen Jung is a clan oligarchic system having gerentocratic characters. The representatives forming the Council essentially come from some definite clans or households. The Sherdukpen *Jung* is dominated by the representatives of the royal clans, the subject clans have their representatives but they are not supposed to play any active role in the Council. The Apatani *Buliang* system is an informal system, and in fact is not a regular Council. Each individual member is called *Buliang* and the Council does not have a separate name.

The *Buliang* as a Council consists of the clan representatives. Every clan has at least one individual *Buliang*. A would-be *Builang* is selected by the existing *Buliang* at a young age and passes through a certain stages of apprenticeship. There are three grades of *Buliangs* in a clan - the eldest *Buliang* known as the *Akha Buliang* is the *Buliang* proper. Then there is the middle aged *Buliang* called the *Yapa Buliang*. He must have been selected by the existing or the preceding *Akha Buliang*, and is ready to take over as the *Akha Buliang*. The *Akha Buliang* position is never increased, a *Yapa Buliang* becomes an *Akha Buliang* only at the death of the existing incumbent. The *Yapa Buliang* may be one or more than one. Then there is the junior or *Ajang Buliang* who is young and future *Yapa* or *Akha Buliang*. He is selected by the *Akha Buliang*. The *Ajang Buliang* may also be one or more than one, and normally after attaining age becomes *Yapa Buliang*. The *Yapa Buliang* and the *Ajang Buliang* actively help the *Akha Buliang* in discharging his duties.

There is no *Kebang* or *Jung* type of a formal or regular body in an Apatani village enjoying control over all the inhabitants of the village. The *Buliangs* are only individual heads of the clan and they together form a somewhat informal council as and when a problem facing the whole village or the tribe is to be solved. Probably because of this informal character of the Council it does not have a local name. The *Buliangs* are only clan representatives and are expected to protect the clan interest.

However in spite of its informal character the Apatani *Buliang* system is successfully maintaining peace and order in the village and among the tribal people. In spite of being the clan representatives, the *Buliangs* are known to rise above their clan interest to promote and protect the interest of the whole village or the tribe. The council does not normally intervene in the individual life of the people or even the disputes between two individuals but when it threatens to affect the whole community it does not hesitate to act as a single authority and to even use force if necessary.

The Apatanis are more individualistic than many other tribes of the state and the *Buliang*'s activities as a Council are kept at a minimum level in the village. The individual *Buliang* deals with the problems of its own clan and even at the clan level personal and petty disputes are left to the concerned individuals to be settled. Retribution for a wrong done is therefore recognised as a means of settling disputes by the Apatanis (as among their neighbours the Nishings). In recent years the influence and authority of the *Buliang* system has further eroded, the government administration and the statutory Panchayats having replaced most of their functions. However, the *Buliangs* still enjoy a superior social position and often settle inter-village disputes or serious disputes between two parties.

The Mockchup System

The Khamti *Mockchup* or *Mukjum* system is the most prominent and most developed among the chieftaincy systems prevalent among the eastern tribes of Arunachal Pradesh. The *Mockchup* (king's council) consists of the Chief, and six members chosen from the subject clans. The Chief as well as the members are chosen by the general assembly of the people. But the Chief must be chosen from the Namchoom clan (royal clan) only. In practice the elders of the royal clan nominate the oldest among the capable in the clan. He is then formally elected by the assembly of the people. However while nominating the Chief his mental and physical capabilities are always taken into consideration. The Khamti Chief is found to be well cultured and well versed with the modern ways of life. He is often an educated wealthy man with experiences of outside world. He is more like a modern prince than a tribal Chief.

The members of the Council are also similarly chosen from different clans including commoners. But in practice some of the memberships have grown hereditary. Of course, the qualifications for the membership of the Council are laid down. It may be mentioned here that the Khamtis are Buddhist and they have their own script. The codes for the Chief and the society are incorporated in their scared book 'the *Thamasat*'.

A Chief is normally chosen for his lifetime. However certain Chiefs in the past are known to have resigned their position on their own. Such ex-Rajas are still called Raja and they enjoy considerable respect in the society. Besides the Chief and his council there are other two officers of the Chief. They are the *Tangsu* (the village messenger who informs the date of trial by the Chief or the decisions of the council to the villagers) and the *Pachai-U* (the messenger carrying information to other villages from the Chief)[10].

The Chief is the head of the council and presides over its meetings. The jurisdiction of the Chief and the Council extends to all Khamti villages[11], and hence the *Mockchup* cannot be called a purely village level institution. It discusses and deliberates upon the matters common to all villages or concerning an individual village. It also settles disputes which cannot be settled by the Village Council at its level. The Chief is to implement the decision of the Council. Theoretically, all land in the Khampti area belongs to him. But he cannot utilise the land and the forest for his personal interest.

Village Level Setup

At the individual village level there is a Chief and a Council in every village. This is called '*Traon*'[12]. The '*Traon*' is subordinate to the '*Mockchup*'. Every '*Traon*' consists of two subordinate Chiefs and a Council. These two Chiefs too come from the Namchoom clan and are chosen by the people of the concerned village. One of them is known as the Old King and the other as the Young King. They are known by different local title in different villages. For example the 'Old King' is known as '*Chowfahop*' in

Moumong village and as *'Chownuhu'* in Kherem village while the 'Young King' is known as *'Chowfakem'* in both the villages. Similarly the members of the Council are also known by different titles in different villages[13].

The village set up looks after all the affairs of the village such as observance of festivals, performance of religious rites, construction of a public house or an irrigation channel, management of funds raised for a particular purpose, arrangement of voluntary labour for constructional or developmental works for implementing Council's decision etc. Its main function is, of course, administration of justice in the village. However if a village level Chief and his Council is unable to solve a problem of the village or fails to settle a disputes it is taken to the Council of the main Chief. Thus the Khamti villages also have their own village level self-governing set up and it performs more or less the same function and plays the same role as the Village Councils prevalent among the other tribes of the state.

The Khamti system too has undergone certain changes in recent years. The Khamtis are one of the most socio-economically advanced tribes of the Arunachal Pradesh. They are found to introduce innovation to their system. For example abandoning the age old practice of electing the oldest eligible person of the royal clan, the Khamtis once elected a young educated person as their Chief. But when it was found that the change did not work to the satisfaction of all due mainly to the attitude of the elders of the royal clan, he was replaced by the eldest member of the clan. At times the Chiefs themselves were found to be more ambitious, trying to rise to state level leadership.

Common Features

In spite of their typological differences, The traditional tribal self governing institutions of Arunachal Pradesh have certain underlying common features. All of them have a gerentocratic tendency and age and experience are respected even in the most democratic form. All of them have certain democratic ethos in their operation and derive their authority from the people. The chieftaincies are of milder form and never autocratic in nature. They even have some element of democracy in them. They always conform to the wishes of the people. Women generally do not take active part in any of the systems.

All the councils are mainly concerned with the administration of justice, and each of them has evolved elaborate mechanism for the purpose. However they also concern themselves with the general administration of the village and developmental activities in the village, although there is a difference in degree in the latter two functions.

All the system operate on spontaneous loyalty of the people and respect for customs and traditions. Decisions are mainly based on unanimity or general consensus, and their implementation depends on their spontaneous execution by the people even by those who are awarded a punishment. Although in the past physical punishment including capital punishment used to be imposed on the wrong doers, now-a-days all punishments awarded by all the systems are in the form of fines.

The Role Played

The traditional tribal self-governing institutions of Arunachal Pradesh played a very important role in the politico-administrative system of the state in the past. The Village Councils of all kinds acted as real village governments well fitting into Sir Charles Metcaff's description of Indian villages as 'little republics' and 'a separate state in itself'[14].

During the British period they were hardly influenced by the British administration. 'The British after their initial extension of administration into the area did not attempt to introduce their system of administration into the entire area. They were largely inclined to follow a policy of isolation by leaving the tribesmen alone. They considered the task of administration in the area difficult and unrewarding. They therefore did not make any attempt to interfere in or greatly modify the functioning of the Village Councils. Instead they tried to administer the countryside through the indigenous system of administration and started the practice of appointing a village headman from among the influential leaders of the traditional Village Councils or a Chief. They also appointed these village headmen (Gaonburhas) as village authorities under the Assam Frontiers (Administration of Justice) Regulation, 1945. This practice virtually amounted to extending official recognition to the Village Councils as village governments, as all Gaonburhas in reality functioned within the framework of the Village Council'.

'After independence, the Government of India followed almost the same policy of isolation towards the tribal people of Arunachal Pradesh. It favoured the policy of retaining the distinctive culture of the tribal people of the area by protecting them from any exogenous influence. The NEFA administration, the forerunner of Arunachal Government, therefore positively encouraged the Village Councils to carry out their functions as before and to develop further wherever necessary'.

'It directed the Political Officers to appoint the traditional Village Councils as village authorities under the 1945 Regulation and to entrust them with development works in the village. These councils therefore continued to function as village governments administering the village, maintaining law and order, carrying out developmental activities and delivering justice in it, even after the independence'.

'The introduction of Panchayati Raj in 1969 shadowed the Village Councils to some extent in certain areas and tended to reduce their role as village governments. But it could not diminish them to any large extent. The failure of the Panchayat Raj Regulation to entrust the Gram Panchayat with any function except electing a member of the Anchal Samiti and its studied silence regarding the traditional Village Councils and an important function hitherto performed by them, traditionally as well as under the Assam Frontier (Administration of Justice) Regulation, 1945, the administration of justice in the village, allowed the traditional Village Councils to continue to perform their role in the village affairs and as a judicial body in the village. Because of its long tradition it continued to exert enough authority and influence in the village even today. True that the working of the statutory panchayats has brought certain changes in their operatives and leadership structure, but they still decide all important issues concerning the village and adjudicate disputes'.[15]

Conclusion

In conclusion it may be said that there are several types of traditional self governing institutions among the tribes of Arunachal Pradesh and they fit into different theoretical models. They are normally village oriented institutions. All the systems invariably include a council of the people or their representatives in one from or the other. The chieftaincies are of milder type and are never autocratic. The Chiefs are often chosen by the people although they come from a particular clan or family. All the types have certain common features in them and function as some sort of a village government. The introduction of the statutory panchayats has affected them to some extent but has not replaced them. They still command respect and spontaneous obedience from the people in almost all the areas. They have vast experience in managing the affaires of the village. They have successfully carried out developmental activities like making a road, building a school house or digging an irrigation channel besides administering justice and maintaining order in the village. They have organised religious performances and village festivals. It is therefore advisable that, the efficiency and experience of these councils be advantageously utilised for purposes of democratic decentralisation and rural development in the state.

Notes and References

1. These tribes (as per Research Department of Arunachal Pradesh) are:

   1. Adi, 2. Apatani, 3. Bangni, 4. Bokar, 5. Bori, 6. Digam Mishmi, 7. Hill Miri, 8. Hrusso (Aka), 9. Idu Mishmi, 10. Khamti, 11. Khamba, 12. Memba, 13. Khawa, 14. Miji, 15. Miju, 16. Monpa, 17. Nishing, 18. Nocte, 19. Sherdukpen, 20. Shingpho, 21. Sulung, 22. Tagin, 23. Tangsha, 24. Pallibo, 25. Ramo, 26. Wangsho.

   Besides there is a sizable population of Mishings and Deoris in Arunachal Pradesh.

2. For a detail discussion, see, P.D. Gogoi, *NEFA Local Polity*, (unpublished-Ph.D. Thesis), II PA, Delhi, 1969, pp. 66-67.

3. The Wangcho Village Council which is dominated by a strong hereditary chieftain does not have an indigenous name. It is loosely called as *Wangsa-Wangso* probably because the Chief invariably calls the Wangsa and Wangsu (two prominent members of the village) to the Council meeting. The council can also be called *'Naopho'* which means assembly. See P.D. Gogoi, ibid, p. 103.

4. The Tangsa Village Council is known by various names like *Mungphong, Nokthung, Khaphva, Khapong, Khapo* etc. ibid., p. 112.

5. The Padams, Minnyiongs, Tasis, Galongs, Mishimgs, Shimongs and the Boris all have more or less a similar system.

6. Verrier Elwin failed to notice this democratic institution of the Nishings. Instead he thought the *Gindung* (the go between) to be the system of self governing set up among the Nishings. Similarly B.K. Shukla, thought the Nishings to be individualistic without any Village Council set up except the *Gindung*. But a recent study carried out by Manosh Kumar, a Rajiv Gandhi Fellow of ISCD reveals the existence and working of Nyile (Village Council) among the Nishings. See, Varrier Elwin, *Democracy in NEFA*, Shillong 1965, B.K. Shukla, *The Daflas of Subansiri*, NEFA Shillong, 1965.

7. See Verrier Elwin, *op cit.*, p. 112 and P.D. Gogoi, *op cit.* p. 119.

8. A.C. Talukdar, *Political Transition in the Grassroots in Tribal India*, Omsons Publications, New Delhi, 1987, pp. 200-201.

9. See P.D. Gogoi, *op. cit.*, pp. 138-139.

10. P.D. Gogoi, *op. cit.*, p. 80.

11. In 1969 there were 12 such villages.

12. P.D. Gogoi, *op. cit.*, p. 79.

13. *ibid.*

14. Sir Charles Mafcaff, quoted by Varrier Elwin, *op. cit.* p. 23.

15. A.C. Talukdar, "Traditional Village Councils of Arunachal Pradesh and their role as village Government", *Journal of North-East India Council for Social Science Research*, Vol. 12, No. 1 (April 1988), pp. 14-15.

9

Traditional Self-Governing Institutions Among the Hill Population Groups of Meghalaya

– L.S. Gassah

The present State of Meghalaya comprises the three major tribal groups of the Khasis, Jaintias and Garos. All these three have their own Autonomous District Councils now. The Autonomous District Councils for the United Khasi-Jaintia Hills District and the Garo Hills District were introduced right from 1952 in accordance with the provision of the Sixth Schedule to the Constitution of India. Subsequently, however, the people of Jaintia Hills felt that a separate District Council was an urgent need for the then Jowai sub-division. A Commission was appointed in 1963 to look into this matter. The Commission recommended for a separate district administration for Jaintia Hills and so a separate District Council for Jaintia Hills was created on the 1st of December 1964 after the bifurcation of the then United Khasi-Jaintia Autonomous District Council. Since then three Autonomous District Councils have been in operation, one each for Khasi Hills, Jaintia Hills and Garo Hills.

The Autonomous District Councils in Meghalaya are such institutions which were introduced among the tribal people of the State only after Independence, to be specific, since 1952. But the tribal people of Meghalaya have their own traditional socio-political institutions since time immemorial. Such institutions are deeply rooted in the society. They can also be considered as traditional self-governing institutions. The traditional institutions were and are still responsible for the day-to-day administration of the people. They run the administration in a democratic manner and in accordance to the general will of the people based on traditions, customs, culture and usages of the land. The traditional Chiefs, though occupy the highest hierarchy in the rung of the ladder of administration, cannot go against the popular will of their people. In many cases, such Chiefs were either selected or elected by the people in order to supervise the administration and not to oppress or suppress them. The people retain the highest authority in matters of decision making although they are helped and guided by the various traditional councils at different levels of administration. These councils play a very important role in the administration and decision making process.

Khasi Hills

Among the Khasis we have the *Syiem* or King at the top of the administration. He is assisted by other officials of the *Hima* or State for the smooth running of the administration. The office of the Khasi *Syiem* emanated as an organ to centralise some common subjects of the administration. The office thus arose out of an impulse for amalgamating identical pursuits, interests and necessities of the clan residents and villagers. It was instituted on the spirit of reciprocity along with a consolidation of their intimate relations which had grown amongst the different sections of people who made up their units.

A Khasi *Syiem* is the head of his State. But he ought to subject himself to ethical instructions, prescribed by customary rules, laws and regulations, as well as customs, traditions and usages. He is the symbol of unity of all the clans and groups of clans and groups of villages within the *Syiemship*. The clans and the villages forming the population of the State, are co-partners with the *Syiem* in the smooth functioning of the entire *Syiemship* administration. He is under the strict control of the whole community. He has to lay down his policy in conformity with the resolution of the *Durbar* (Council) of the people. The *Durbars* actually transacted both the political and judicial matters and their decision is final. The acts or decisions of a *Syiem* can be vetoed by the *Durbar* if they are contrary to the usages and traditions of the community. A *Syiem* is always assisted by his *Myntris* (Ministers) in all matters concerning the *Syiemship* administration. In judicial matters or in the administration of justice, a *Syiem* acts as a judge and the *Durbar* as a jury.

The sovereignty of the Khasi State is based on customary laws of the Khasi people established since the inception of the society and handed down from generation to generation. This sovereignty further reflected by the general will of the people as may be exercised and expressed by them from time to time. The *Syiem* exercises civil, judicial and executive powers; in the past the *Syiem's* court was the highest court of appeal within his *Syiemship*, although his authority was derived from and exercised by the State *Durbars* (Councils) sitting in judgement in his presence, and the verdict in his name is in actuality a resolution and agreement of a *Durbar*. In all his executive actions, he was advised by a *Durbar* of *Myntries* (Council of Ministers). His executive action today extends principally to management of markets, arrest of wrong-doers and criminals and collection of fines and imposts at various quarters in the State. He also approves the appointment of subordinate officials of the State.

The *Syiem*'s position is that of a nominal Chief; he is simply an elected head and his tenure of office is limited to his people's pleasure. That the *Syiem*'s powers are limited and circumscribed can be envisaged from the constitutional, legal, social and religious checks and restraints imposed by the usages and convenants upon him. He cannot override the decision of his ministers and those of the State and local councils. Legally, he has no power to make laws or impose fresh levies or issue ordinance. In all acts of legislation he and his State *Durbar* make laws but such laws should in all ordinary cases conform to the usage and customs of the land.

Jaintia Hills

The Jaintias too have their own traditional political institutions. These institutions played a very crucial role in the process of self management of the people as they were also responsible in looking after the socio-economic welfare of the people.

At the much earlier period of time, the Jaintias were under the administration and leadership of *U Langdoh* or priest, both at the village and groups of villages or *Raid.* The *Langdoh* combined in himself both the sacred or religious and secular functions. The first incumbent of the office of the priest of the *Raid* was elected from among the priestly families of the villages of the *Raid.* But with the increase in the number of families and clans, area and size of population, there was also an increase in the number or duties and functions to be performed single-handedly by the *Langdoh.* This led to the general feeling among the inhabitants that the administrative set up should be restructured. As a result, it was felt necessary to bifurcate the dual functions of sacred and secular affairs which were under the power and authority of the *Langdoh.* In the process, it was decided to hand over those functions which were purely sacred in nature to the priest and the other functions which were purely administrative or secular to the secular Chief, *U Doloi* or Provincial Governor. Thus, the office of the *Doloi* in Jaintia Hills came into existence.

U Doloi is therefore the Chief of the next higher political unit called *Elaka* or Province, which was formed by combining a group of villages or *Raid.* Once a *Doloi* takes up his office, he normally holds it for the rest of his life. But he may be punished, expelled or stripped of his office, should he arouse sufficient hostility to his people. The powers and functions of the *Dolois* are therefore circumscribed by the society which differentiates them from other Chiefs prevailing among other tribal communities of the region, especially those outside Meghalaya.

A *Doloi* is the administrative head of an *Elaka*. He exercises his functions within the jurisdiction of his *Elaka*. The *Dolois* in Jaintia Hills are not autocratic rulers and have no dictatorial power over the people of their respective *Elakas*. Their provinces are really republics though very tiny indeed. Like the *Syiem*, when this office was in existence in Jaintia Hills, the *Dolois* also have to run the administration according to the popular opinion of their *Elakas*. This is clearly noticed from the fact that all actions initiated or taken by a *Doloi* are to be approved by all the citizens of the *Elaka*, through the general *Durbar* of the *Raid* or *Elaka*.

The *Dolois* in Jaintia Hills had certain executive, political, judicial and religious functions to perform within their respective jurisdiction. In the past, they also performed military functions. Besides extending their hands to the *Syiem* in his administration, the *Dolois* on their part executed and exercised important decisions in matters relating to the administration and welfare of the people of their *Elakas*. In running the administration of his *Elaka*, the *Doloi* was and is still assisted and guided by the *Durbar Elaka* or *Durbar Raid* and an executive council of leading persons like the *Pator* (Lt. Governor), clan representatives and others.

Garo Hills

In Garo Hills, the institution of *Nokmaship* and the Village Council were the two traditional administrative agencies. The institution of *Nokmaship* is as old as the first settlement of the Garos in the Garo Hills.

The Garos entered the present Garo Hills in batches from different directions, each batch consisting of a clan and each clan settling in a particular area. The leader of the clan who has thus brought his people and settled them in a particular area of the Garo Hills was automatically recognised as their leader or headman called *Nokma* in Garo language. But the *Nokma* does not enjoy autocratic powers as all the decisions are taken at a joint assembly of all the elders of the village. With the passage of time, there evolved various types of *Nokmas* in the Garo Hills. Of these, only the *A'king Nokma* has the political and administrative power. A man becomes the *A'king Nokma* by virtue of his relationship to the woman who is the head of the village community. Such a man is generally the husband of the senior-most woman of the clan but other relatives are sometimes appointed for special reasons. The *A'king Nokma* is not the proprietor of the land but the representative of the woman who is the head of the clan or the village community, and she is not the proprietor of the village but the head of the village community who is the owner. As the head of the clan and as the custodian of the *A'king* land, he is entrusted with certain political and administrative powers. As such, it is the only type of *Nokma* who possesses certain political and administrative powers.

A long traditional custom endows certain rights and privileges to the *A'king Nokma.* Breach of these privileges amounts to a usurpation and an insolence to the *Nokma.* Among these, the most important single characteristic of the *A'king Nokma* is the possession of titles to land. Titles to *A'king* land can be bought or sold to others, but sale or purchase can be done only with the full consent of his wife and her *charas* or her maternal uncles and brothers. Thus title to some lands is a necessary prerequisite for being considered a *Nokma,* though title to land alone is not enough. Therefore, it will be found that though the office of the *Nokma* has no obvious privileges, it is by no means a completely unattractive position as a certain amount of prestige is attached with the office.

The *A'king Nokma* occupies a high place in the Garo society. This office has an intrinsic importance from the point of view of the Garo organisation. It is the pivot of the village organisation through which the basic network of the entire society is woven. In fact, the *Nokma* plays the leading role as the central figure in the village activities and externally represents the village. However, the position of the *Nokma* is very delicate. In fact, the *Nokma* cannot be compared to a Chief who exercises his authority with various social and economic advantages. The *Nokma* is rather a social and economic representative of the village without having any advantage or authority in the true sense of the term.

The *A'king Nokma's* economic status is basically equal to that of others. Though the *A'king* land belongs to the wife of the *Nokma,* it is actually held in common by all the inhabitants of the village. Every member of the village has the right to cultivate the village land. The possession of the *A'king* land is simply represented by the *Nokma's* wife and managed by the *Nokma.* As a rule, no portion of the *A'king* land can be sold or mortgaged by the *Nokma.* The village land is divided into several parts on the basis of annual rotation of jhum cultivation. Every year one of these parts is distributed to each household, and the share of the *Nokma's* family is allotted in the same way as that of other families. In fact, the *Nokma* receives one direct economic benefit form his title, though it is very insignificant, that is, an annual fee called *A'will,* paid by an outsider if he wants to cultivate land within the *A'king* land.

The *A'king Nokma* is the centre of social activities within the village and outside. He is also responsible for the peace and good administration within his *A'king* land. He has to keep himself abreast of all that is going on within his jurisdiction. He has also to regulate jhum cultivation, which is one of his important duties, and participate with the villagers in all public and social works and functions. In olden days, it devolved upon the *Nokma* to lead his people to wars and to protect his village against external invasions.

In the settlement of disputes, the *Nokma* tried all cases, both civil and criminal, committed within his *A'king* land, with the help of the elders and of the village in an open court. Decisions were made either by conciliations or by imposing fines as compensations which is called *Dai* on the guilty. Their decisions were final and were put into execution at once. Thus, it is clear that under the traditional system, the clan or *Ma'chong* was the socio-political unit and there could be no authority above that of the *Nokma* who managed the affairs of the clan with the consent of the people.

Under the British rule, the powers and functions of the *Nokmas* were greatly reduced. The Regulation X of 1882 legalised the Draft Proposals of David Scott, according to which a *Laskar* and *Sardar* were to be appointed oven ten or twelve villages, which means an appointment or a *Laskar* and *Sardar* over a certain number of *A'king Nokmas*. A *Laskar* is an elective head of a group of villages called *Elaka* which are united for fiscal and administrative purposes, each village being under its hereditary *Nokma*. The Scheduled Districts Act, 1874, conferred on the *Laskar* some powers in matters of Police, Civil and Criminal justice and in revenue administration within his *Elaka*. They were also empowered to impose a fine whereas the *A'king Nokmas* were to collect revenue of his village, collect revenue of his village, maintain law and order in it, report all crimes to the *Laskar* and arrest the offenders.

Under the District Council administration, the *A'king Nokmas* have been reduced to mere custodians and supervisors of their *A'kings* on behalf of their wives and their clans. However, the Garo Hills District (Jhum) Regulation, 1954, conferred on the *A'king Nokmas* the right to allot land for jhuming to each family within his *A'king* in consultation with the residents thereof. But in the event of any dispute with regard to the land so allotted by the *A'king Nokma* to any particular persons or a family, the matter has to be referred to the Village Council, a power which was exercised by the *A'king Nokma* before.

With regard to the trial of cases over which the *A'king Nokma* used to preside over since time immemorial, his powers have been taken away by the passing of the Garo Hills Autonomous District (Administration of Justice) Rules, 1953. According to this Act, there are three classes of Courts, namely, the Village Court, Subordinate District Council Court and the District Council Court. These Courts try all civil and criminal cases falling within the purview of tribal laws and customs in which both the parties belong to Scheduled Tribes and are the residents within its jurisdiction. With regard to the powers of administration and general supervision of the *Nokmas* within his *A'king* land, his powers have been taken away by the Village Councils by passing of the Garo Hills District (Constitution of Village Councils) Acts, 1958, whose members are elected.

The above brief discussion on the socio-cultural, ecological and political-economic roots of self-management of the tribal people of Meghalaya brings into focus the strong link between the traditional socio-political institutions and the people themselves. We have noticed how those traditional institutions play their role in maintaining not only law and order but their active participation in the economic uplift of the people within their respective jurisdiction. Many of such traditional institutions were responsible in the regulation and distribution of jhum lands so that each family or household has a plot of land for cultivation. A Chief would not like to see his people suffer from shortage of food, unless some unnatural forces take their own course. It was the duty of the Chief to ensure that every family or household gets a plot of land to cultivate.

Evidently, the powers of the traditional Chiefs in Khasi, Jaintia and Garo Hills had been threatened by the new administrative set up since India's independence. The stepping of the District Council into the shoes of either the traditional institutions or the British and post-independence constitutional authorities, did not bring any improvement in the power position of the traditional Chiefs. On the contrary, the new power structure has radically reduced the powers of the Chiefs. Moreover, on many occasions, there have been tussles between the traditional elite represented by the Chiefs and the modern political elite (popular elected representatives). On one pretext or another the Chiefs might be suspended or even dismissed by the District Council on charges like insubordination, mal-practices and disobedience. This tussle is a continuing affair.

The traditional Chiefs are now treated by the District Council as its subordinate officials. The Chiefs and headmen are completely under the control and supervision of the District Council. Under the provision of paragraph, 3(I) (g) of the Sixth Schedule, the Indian Constitution has empowered it to make laws with respect to the appointment or succession of Chiefs or headmen. The United Khasi-Jaintia Hills Autonomous District (Appointment and Succession of Chiefs and Headmen) Act, 1959, made provision not only for its authority to appoint the Chiefs and Headmen, but also the removal and suspension of the same by the Executive Committee of the District Council if in its opinion these incumbents violated the terms and conditions of their appointment. This Act not only brought radical changes in the pattern and procedure of the election and appointment of Chiefs, but reduced their position and status, and the District Council even treated them as its 'administrative heads'. At one point of time, the District Council even suggested to the State Government not to correspond with the traditional Chiefs directly. It is therefore obvious that such actions taken by the District Council had created resentment between the traditional and modern institutions. Thus the relationship between the traditional Chiefs and that of the District Council has been all along under strains. The Supreme Court in 1960 in the case of T. Cajee, Chief Executive Member of the United Khasi-Jaintia Hills Autonomous District Council *versus U.* Jormanik Syiem, the *Syiem* of Mylliem, observed that "the position, after the coming into force of the Constitution was that the Chiefs lost whatever ruling or administrative powers they had with the merger of these twenty five states (Khasi States) in Assam and the governance of these States was to be carried on according to the provisions of the Sixth Schedule". Paradoxically, these new situations during the transitional period are a threat to the traditional institutions and democratic practices of the people. It may even be said that with the dawn of independence and especially with the setting up of the District Council, the period of an 'erosion of democracy' in the area begins. Such new political institutions which were created after independence were in fact eroding the powers and functions of traditional councils instead of improving them.

The District Council appears not only to be alien to the traditional institutions, but the powers and functions of the traditional Chiefs have been threatened due to its existence in the area. Because of this reason, the District Council was never welcomed by the traditional Chiefs. The stepping of the District Council into the shoes of either the Jaintia *Raja* or the British and Indian authorities did not bring any improvement in the power position of the Chiefs. On the contrary, the new power structure had radically reduced their powers. For example, the United Khasi-Jaintia Hills Autonomous District (Appointment and Succession of Chiefs and Headmen) Act, 1959 (hereinafter referred to as the Principal Act), introduced two fundamental changes from the traditional customary practices of the people as per Sections 10 and 11 which relate to the appointment of deputy Chief (Section 10) and an acting Chief (Section 11). The Jaintia Hills Autonomous District Council which was established in 1964, adopted the Principal Act as it is during its initial years of existence. In the subsequent years, this District Council made certain amendments to the Principal Act. For example, the Jaintia Hills Autonomous District Council passed an amendment Act in 1973 which deleted the entire Section 10 of the Principal Act relating to the appointment of deputy Chief. The District Council realised the uselessness and inapplicability of such a provision of the Act and more importantly it shows the complete deviation from the traditional customary practices of the people. However, the Executive Committee of the Jaintia Hills District Council still retains Section 11 of the Principal Act relating to the appointment of an acting Chief. Armed with this constitutional power, the Executive Committee of the said Council appointed a number of acting *Dolois* from time to time, either after the death, removal or suspension of the regular *Doloi* in an *Elaka*. Such appointment of an acting Chief has been criticized as it represents complete deviation from the traditional customary practice of appointing an acting Chief. A Chief once appointed, holds the office for life, unless removed for very strong reasons, like moral turpitude or commission of heinous crimes. Moreover, according to the traditional customary practices, a Chief must be a person belonging to the particular clan or clans chosen from time immemorial. No other clans in the society not enjoying this particular privilege have the right to setting up of candidates for the office of *Doloi*. But according to the aforesaid Section (Section 11) of the Principal Act, it is mentioned very specifically that the Executive Committee of the District Council may appoint "any person" who could be from any clan to act as an acting Chief and exercise all the powers and functions of the Chief. This step taken by the District Council is sure to create confusion in the minds of the people. It also shows a complete deviation from the traditional practices and against the norms of the society.

The traditional Chiefs being treated by the District Council as its subordinate officials, are accountable for their actions to it. They have been directed to desist from criticism of the functioning of the Executive Committee of the District Council in any form. The Chiefs are also debarred to participate in any demonstration or resort to any form of strike in connection with any matter pertaining to their condition of service. These conditions laid down by the District Council gave rise to suspicion and mistrust between the two institutions. Likewise, the various Acts enforced from time to time by the District Council under the Sixth Schedule to the Constitution brought radical changes in the pattern and procedure of election and appointment or succession of Chiefs and Headmen in Khasi and Jaintia Hills Districts of Meghalaya.

Thus, under the new constitutional set up, the Chiefs are pushed behind the line of leadership. They are to keep themselves content with whatever power and functions left to them by the District Council. Though the District Council granted certain unofficial pickings to the Chiefs, it however reduced them to a much lesser status. In the District Council's dealing with the Chiefs, there is a strong feeling that it has not fully appreciated their continuance as desirable traditional institutions and the Chiefs are treated as personalities or individuals of their respective *Elakas* and villages. This naturally leads to different or discriminatory treatments of adhoc nature without a firm and definite policy of preserving the institutions in their pristine purity. This has also caused a sense of confusion among the people in general, a feeling of uncertainty, if not of mistrust or suspicion among the Chiefs of the motive of the District Council as to their continuance as custodians and trustees of the customs and traditions of the people.

References

1. H. Bareh, *The History and Culture of the Khasi People,* 1967.
2. Milton, S. Sangma, *History and Culture of the Garos,* 1981.
3. L.S. Gassah (Ed.), *Garo Hills : Land and the People,* 1984.
4. B.L. Hansaria, *Sixth Schedule to the Constitution of India: A Study,* 1983.
5. *Constituent Assembly of India Debates,* Vol. IX, 1949.
6. *The Khasi Hills Autonomous District Council Acts, Rules, Regulations,* etc.
7. *The Jaintia Hills Autonomous District Council Acts, Rules, Regulations,* etc.
8. *The Garo Hills Autonomous District Council Acts, Rules, Regulations,*_etc.
9. L.S. Gassah, 'The Sixth Schedule to the Constitution of India', *North-Eastern Hill University* (General Foundation Course), 1983.
10. L.S. Gassah, 'Relevance of the Sixth Schedule in Meghalaya', *News and Views,* 1986.
11. L.S. Gassah, 'Pattern of Economic Change in Jaintia Society', *The NEHU Journal of Social Sciences and Humanities,* Vol. VIII, No. 4, Oct. - Dec., 1990.

10

Traditional Self-Governing Institutions Among the Hill Tribal Population Groups of Assam

– *B.N. Bordoloi*

When we speak of tribal areas of Assam, we refer to the two autonomous hill districts of Assam, viz., Karbi Anglong and North Cachar Hills. As per Assam Scheduled Castes and Scheduled Tribes Amendment Act, 1976, there are 14 ethnic groups which are enlisted as Scheduled Tribes in the hill areas of Assam and these are as follows:

1. Chakma, 2. Dimasa Kachari, 3. Garo, 4. Hajong, 5. Hmar, 6. Khasi, Jaintia, Synteng, Phar, War, Bhoi, Lyngngam, 7. Any Kuki Tribes (37 sub-groups), 8. Lakher, 9. Man (Tai-speaking), 10. Any Mizo (Lushai) Tribes, 11. Mikir, 12. Any Naga Tribes, 13. Pawi, 14. Syntheng.

As per 2001 census, of the total population of Assam is 224.14 lakh and the number of hill tribal population is 4.40 lakh constituting 1.96 per cent of the state's total population.

It is also very interesting to note that the scheduled tribe population in these two hill districts constitutes 54.65 per cent of the total tribal population of the state. As per 2001 census the tribal population in the district of Karbi Anglong and North Cachar Hills stands at 52.06 and 66.44 per cent respectively.

In this paper the traditional self-governing institutions which are still prevalent among some of the tribal communities inhabiting the hill areas of Assam are taken up for discussion.

Since the Karbis are the largest tribal group in the hill areas of Assam, let us take up for discussion the traditional self-governing institutions among them first.

Traditional Self-governing Institutions Among the Karbis of the Karbi Anglong District

The Karbis of the Karbi Anglong district have a three-tier traditional self-governing institution. At the apex there is the 'king' of Rongkhang area called *Lingdokpo* and his Parliament or Council of Officers called *Pinpomar*. At the middle level there are 12 *Habais* or administrators one each for 12 *Longris* to which the entire traditional 'Karbi kingdom' is divided. A *Longri* consists of several contiguous Karbi villages. Each of the 12 *Longris* has a Council of Officers and this Council presided over by the concerned *Habai* is called *Longri-A-Mei*. At the village level there is the traditional village headman called *Sarthe*. There is also a village Council called *Mei* and this Council is presided over by the *Sarthe*.

However, this traditional three-tier self-governing institution has now been found to be operative in the Hamren Sub-division only of the Karbi Anglong district. In the other sub-division, that is, Diphu, the first two tiers, viz., the *Lingdokpo*ship and *Habai*ship have become defunct. Of course, the third tier, that is to say, *Sarthe*ship and the village council *Mei* has been functioning there with limited activities.

(a) *Lingdokpo (Kingship)*

In the Hamren sub-division there are three traditional local kings with their territorial jurisdiction at Rongkhang, Cinthong and Amri. Although they are now, in fact, tribal Chiefs only, we are using the term king here since the people themselves call them *Lingdokpo* which literally means a king. Hamren sub-division has three tribal development blocks, i.e., Rongkhang, Cinthong and Amri and these three development blocks coincide with the territorial divisions of the three Karbi kings. In Karbi language a king is called *Lingdokpo* or *Resho*.

Among the three *Lingdokpos*, Rongkhang *Lingdokpo* is considered to be supreme from the point of view of hierarchy. He is very often referred to as Karbi *Resho*. Next to him is the Cinthong *Lingdokpo* and the *Lingdokpo* of Amri occupies the lowest position.

The traditional capital of the Karbis being located at Niz Rongkhong, a village situated about 20 km away from Hamren, the sub-divisional head quarters of Hamren-Sub-division, the Rongkhang *Lingdokpo* lives here and that is why, this village is known as Raja Gaon also.

Each of the three principal *Lingdokpos* of Rongkhang, Chinthong and Amri has a number of subordinate *Lingdokpos*. The Tongkhang *Lingdokpo* has three subordinate Chiefs, namely, *Rongchaicho Lingdokpo, Killing Lingdokpo* and *Rongpi Lingdokpo*. The *Cingthong Lingdokpo* has two subordinate Chiefs called *Nonglada Lingdokpo* and *Nongpli Lingdokpo*. Similarly *Amri Lingdokpo* has also two subordinate Chiefs known as *Du Lingdokpo* and *Nongkirla Lingdokpo*.

(b) Pinpomar or Council of Functionaries

The traditional administration is run by the *Ronghang Lingdokpo* with the help of a Parliament or a Council called *Pinpomar* constituted with the highest level functionaries. *Bardili*, the principal functionary who may be regarded as the Prime Minister, *Katharbura* or the priest, *Pator,* who assists *Bardili* in all matters and *Dengja,* the adviser to the king in respect of spiritual matters, are the seniormost functionaries of the *Pinpomar*.

(c) Selection of Lingdokpos

A *Lingdokpo,* whether be it of Rongkhang, Cinthong or Amri, is democratically selected by the people with the assistance of the concerned *Pinpomar*. The Karbi kingship has never been hereditary. However, the king could be selected from Ronghang sub-clan only; the Cinthong *Lingdokpo* must be selected from Hanse sub-clan only and the Amri *Lingdokpo* must be selected from also from Hanse sub-clan.

A king could be deposed or dismissed by the people if he is considered to be inefficient in running the administration or if he is found to be guilty of incest or if he is lacking in judicious judgements in trying cases.

Shri Sarman Ronghang who became the *Lingdokpo* of Rongkhang in 1976 and whom I met in Niz Rongkhang in August 1983 was already deposed due to his inefficiency as well as quarrelsome habits although he was physically fit to continue in the post. The people selected Shri Kat Ronghang as their new *Lingdokpo* in 1990. In selecting a new king the people pay due consideration to the following qualities of the concerned person :

(i) He must be well conversant with all the customary laws of the Karbi society;

(ii) He must be physically and mentally fit to hold the august office and must possess the qualities of a leader;

(iii) He must be a man of high moral character and integrity with a commanding personality; and

(iv) Lastly, he must be a well-behaved man with an amiable disposition and gifted with judicious decision-making ability.

Thus there is no chance for a Karbi *Lingdokpo* to be an autocrat and the fear that he could be deposed of at any time, controls his actions and decisions.

(d) Pinpomar and its Members

The *Pinpomar*, which is the council of highest level officials or functionaries, consists mainly of *Bardili, Katharbura* and *Dengja*.

(i) *Bardili* is the principal executive functionary of the king. As such he is not only the right hand person of the king but the most trustworthy officer too. In fact it is the *Bardili* who performs all the activities of the traditional Karbi kingdom on behalf of the king and he is also the spokesman of the king.

Like the *Lingdokpo*, the *Bardili* is also selected by the people and thus this post is not hereditary. In order to be eligible for the post of *Bardili*, certain conditions must be satisfied.

(a) He must be a man from the *Terang* clan.

(b) He must be a married man.

(c) His wife must be either from the *Tisso* or *Rongpi* sub-clan of *Inghi* sub-clan.

Bardili has an assistant called *Pator* who assists and helps the Chief functionary in all matters.

(ii) The highest priesthood under a *Lingdokpo* is vested in the *Kathar* family only from *Ingti* clan. The priest of the king is called *Katharbura* and he performs worship once in a year on 9th and 10th March not only for peace and prosperity of the Karbi community but for the entire humankind as well. *Katharbura* also acts as the adviser to the king in respect of all religious matters.

(iii) Another important functionary of the *Pinpomar* is *Dengja*. He must be a man from the *Teron* clan and during the bygone days his duty was to make the human sacrifice once in a year. It is reported that the last human sacrifice was made in 1965. The assistant of the *Dengja* is called *Miji*. These two officials have practically no functions except offering advice to the king on spiritual maters.

Assigned Duties of the Functionaries of Pinpomar

The functionaries of the *Pinpomar* have well assigned duties.

While the *Bardili* assisted by the *Patar* attends to all social matters and settles all the disputes referred to the king by the *Habais* and other *Lingdokpo*, all the religious matters are looked after by the *Katharbura*. He is, of course, helped by the *Dengja* and *Miji* whenever required. When a *Habai* settles any dispute, the *Lingdokpo* has to be informed immediately with a bottle of *Horlang* (rice beer). If the king is satisfied with the judgement delivered by the *Habai*, the case is considered settled. Otherwise the king may ask *Bardili* to have a second look at it. If the *Bardili* finds it difficult to arrive at a judicious decision in settling a case, it is referred to the king and the judgement delivered by him is final.

But there is a supreme appellate tribunal also called *Arnampharo-A-Mei* or Council of wisemen consisting of wise men drawn from different clans and sub-clans which may overrule the decisions not only of a *Bardili* but the decision of a king too.

The *Lingdokpo* and his wife whom the common Karbis regard as their queen, live like common people and cultivate their own *Jhum* fields and their residence has no special feature. But once in a year the royal *Darbar* is held in the village where the *Lingdokpo* lives under the shade of a big tree. On the *Darbar* day the king and the queen as well as the members of the *Pinpomar* are paid tributes generally in kind by the *Habais* and other officials of the *Longris, Sarthes* and other common people who come to attend the *Darbar*. However, the quantum of tribute to be paid is not fixed.

The *Lingdokpo* and the *Pinpomar* have now no political powers since such powers vested in them by the people in the past are now exercised by the Karbi Anglong District Council. But so far as the traditional social, religious and judicial aspects are concerned, the *Lingdokpo* and the *Pinpomar* have been discharging their duties till today. as done in the past, among the Karbis of the Hamren sub-division who have not yet accepted Christianity.

(e) Habai and Longri-A-Mei

We have mentioned earlier that the ancient Karbi kingdom was divided into 12 administrative units called *Longri*. The administrator of a *Longri* is called *Habai*. *A Habai* of a *Longri* is appointed by the concerned *Lingdokpo*. But the king has the however to dismiss him when he is found (1) disloyal or disobedient to the *Pinpomar*, (2) becomes physically unfit due to sudden accident, (3) marries more than one wife, (4) delays the trials of some cases under this or that pretext and (5) embraces Christianity.

Although the *Habai* is the head of the administration of a *Longri*, nevertheless, in discharging his duties a Regional Council called *Longri-A-Mei*, helps him. This Council consists of the following members :

(I) *Habai Kong* (Principal *Habai*)

(II) *Habai Riso* (Assistant *Habai* who must be younger in age)

(III) *Brutrmen* (Expert in traditional laws)

(IV) *Mutlar* (Organising Secretary)

(V) *Hemai* (Assistant to *Mutlar*)

(VI) *Basapo* (One who arranges the sittings of the *Longri-A-Mei*)

(VII) *Pherenke* (Messenger)

(VIII) *Sarthes* (Headmen of the villages under the jurisdiction of a *Longri*).

The *Habai* with the help of the *Longri-A-Mei* decides and settles all the disputes within the *Longri* which are referred to him. When he fails to decide or settle a dispute he refers it to the *Lingdokpo* for final decision. In fact, he is the custodian of all traditional laws and social practices, and he, therefore, must be a wise and experienced man fully conversant with the customs, traditions and social practices of the Karbi society.

The *Habai* is also directly responsible for the maintenance of law and order and also peace and tranquillity within the *Longri*.

Except the *Sarthes*, the other officials of the *Longri-A-Mei* are appointed by the concerned *Lingdokpo* on the advice of the *Habai*. It would not be out of place to mention here that the *Habai* of a *Longri* is the most respected and honoured man within it.

The *Habai* also settles inter-village disputes within the *Longri*, unsettled or undecided disputes referred to him by the *Sarthes*, imposes fines and other punishments on the guilty as per Karbi customary laws and so on. The *Habai* must obey the directives of the *Pinpomar* and he must actively participate in all the community festivals for which he must be invited well ahead.

The *Habai*ship is hereditary. But if a *Habai* dies or if he is dismissed by the *Lingdokpo* and if he is sonless, the *Lingdokpo* appoints a suitable male member as *Habai* from the same clan.

(f) Sarthe and Mei

So far as the village level administration is concerned, the *Sarthe* appointed by the *Habai* of the concerned *Longri*, is at the top of a traditional Karbi village. *Sarthe* literally means the village headman. The *Sartheship* is not hereditary. Nor there is any customary law that the *Sarthe* of a village must be a man belonging to a particular clan or sub-clan. The *Sarthes* of traditional Karbi village can be dismissed by the *Habai* on ground of inefficiency and incompetence. It is very interesting to mention here that a Karbi village is named after the village headman and, therefore along with appointment of a new village headman, the name of the village gets automatically changed. The post of the *Sarthe* is a coveted one. No community festival in the village can take place without his approval. In any social gathering within the village he has to be given the most honoured place. While offering rice-beer, the first treat must go to him. In the trial of cases whenever any fine is imposed on the guilty, the lion's share would go to him. This post being so much lucrative, sometimes a part of a big village is shifted to a new site where the person which leads such an expedition becomes the new *Sarthe* of the hamlet.

The *Sarthe* has the full control over all the socio-religious and judicial matters within the jurisdiction of the village. But the *Sarthe* cannot try any cases relating to sex offences and murder. Such crimes committed within a Karbi village have to be referred to the concerned *Habai* of the *Longri*. Now-a-days, in a Karbi village there is also the village headman appointed by the Karbi Anglong District Council. But of the two, *Sarthe*, the traditional headman, commands more respect and traditionally his post carries more weight though he receives no monetary compensation for the services rendered.

In discharging his duties, the *Sarthe* is helped by a Council of village elders called *Mei*. All adult males of a village are the members of the *Mei*. One of the principal functions of *Mei* is to select sites for shifting cultivation which is known as *Jhum* in north east India, distribute *Jhum* plots among the families of the village and also decide as to whether the village would be shifted to the new *Jhum* site.

However, the Mikir Hill District (Jhumming) Regulation, 1954 and its subsequent amendment in 1966 have curtailed some of the important activities of the village council or *Mei* so far as the shifting of villages to new *Jhum* sites, selection of new Jhum sites and allotment of Jhum plots to individual families are concerned. Now as per provisions of the above Regulation as amended up-to-date, shifting of villages has been totally prohibited. Formerly the Karbi villages had no boundaries. But this Regulation provides for fixation of boundaries of each village.

Secondly, powers entrusted to the village council by the community in respect of management of Jhum sites like rotation, selection of *Jhum* sites, allotment of *Jhum* plots to individual families of the village keeping in view the actual requirement of each family and its capability, have now been taken away and vested with the concerned *Mauzadar* and the *Sarkari Gaonbura* of the village appointed by the Karbi Anglong District Council.

Barring the matters mentioned above, the Karbi Anglong District Council does not interfere with the activities as well as customary rights and privileges enjoyed by the three-tier traditional self-governing institutions still prevalent among the Karbis.

Participation of Women

In the three-tier traditional self-governing institutions, the Karbi women have virtually no space at all. They neither hold any portfolio in the *Pinpomar, Longri-A-Mei* and the and the *Mei* nor they are allowed to participate in their sittings. In the trial of cases of course, if some women are involved, the concerned woman or women are required attend the trial sessions. On the annual *Darbar* day, when the *Lingdokpo* acts as the actual king, the queen, meaning the wife of *Lingdokpo,* who also attends the *Darbar* along with the king, but does not participate in the discussions held there. Nevertheless, she is held in high esteem.

Similarly, the wife of the *Habai* called *Habai Sikopo* is also highly respected by one and all within a *Longri.* However, she, like the queen, *Lingdokpo*'s wife, cannot participate in any discussion held by the *Longri-A-Mei* which is presided over by the *Habai,* her husband.

2. Traditional Self-Governing Institutions Among the Dimasa Kacharies of North Cachar Hills District

Salis or Village Council

The traditional self-governing institution among the Dimasa Kacharis of the North Cachar hills district is found to exist at present only at the village level. It is the village council called *Salis* in Dimasa which literally means a society court. The *Salis* is headed by *Khunang,* the traditional village headman. The post of the *Khunang* is not hereditary. All the adult males of a village are the members of the village council, *Salis.* But whenever a new *Khunang* is selected at the death of the present *Khunang,* only the elder male members of the village participate in such a process. The village elders can also dismiss or depose of the *Khunang* of a village at any time on some specific grounds.

Khunang is the most powerful man in a Dimasa Kachari village. From the point of view of age and experience he should be the seniormost person in the village, By virtue of being the head of the village council, he is also the village headman. He has both executive and judicial powers. His executive powers consist mainly of giving guidance in respect of celebration of community festivals, while his judicial powers consist of trying cases and maintenance of law and order in the village. Besides the *Khunang,* there are 7 (seven) officials in the village council and they are

Dilek, Daulathu, Habaisagao, Pharai, Mantri, Hangsebukhu and *Jalairao*. While *Khunang, Dilek, Daulathu, Habaisagao* and *Pharai* make the senior group, the remaining three officials, namely, *Mantri, Hangsebukhu* and *Jalairao* form the junior group. The five officials of the senior group including the *Khunang* are selected by the village elders (males only) in a formal meeting and the three members of the junior group are selected by the members of the senior group and as such the latter group is virtually under the full control of the senior group.

Dilek is the assistant headman of a Dimasa Kachari village and he assists the *Khunang* in all activities.

Next to *Dilek* is the official called *Daulathu* who must be younger to *Dilek* in age. *Habaisao* who comes next holds office only for two years. Then comes *Pharai*.

So far as the junior group is concerned, except *Jalairao*, the other two officials, namely, *Mantri* and *Hangsebukhu* are no longer in existence now in the present day Dimasa society.

Being the traditional headman of the village, *Khunang* is well-conversant with the customs, traditions and traditional laws of the Dimasa Kacharis and wields considerable authority. In fact, his authority is undisputed so far as the affairs of the village are concerned. He is also respected by one and all in the village.

The traditional village council with eight functionaries headed by the *Khunang* settles disputes, tries cases of theft, incests, divorce, elopement, etc., and the judgements delivered by it must be abided by all the parties concerned. When women are involved, the elderly women are also invited to participate in the trials. In case of inter-village disputes, the *Khunang*s of different villages along with some senior functionaries sit together and settle them. If no agreement is arrived at, the matter is referred to the North Cachar Hills District Council Court for final settlement.

Another important fact is that no community festival in a Dimasa Kachari village could be performed without the prior approval of the *Khunang*.

Let us now examine whether the emergence of the North Cachar Hills District Council has strengthened or weakened the effectiveness of the *Salis*, the traditional village council of the Dimasa Kacharis.

Khunang is recognised by the North Cachar Hills District Council authority as the headman of a Dimasa Kachari village. In addition to his responsibility of maintaining the law and order situations in the village and the trial of cases, N.C. Hills District Council has entrusted him with some additional responsibilities like the collection of house tax and agricultural tax, maintenance of birth and death register, maintenance of records of arms in the village, etc. Moreover, the *Khunang* is made responsible for execution of all developmental programmes meant for implementation in his village. As the Dimasa society is mostly guided by customs and traditions, the additional responsibility now shouldered by the *Khunang* does not stand in his way of discharging his traditional functions. This has rather added to the powers and functions of the traditional village council in an indirect manner.

Participation of Women

The Dimasa Kachari women are not allowed to participate in the discussions of the *Salis* except in trial of cases where women are involved. In such situations the elderly women of a Dimasa Kachari village attend the trial of cases and actively participate in the deliberations.

3. Traditional Self-governing Institutions Among the Hmars of the North Cachar Hills District of Assam

The *Hmars* of the North Cachar Hills district of Assam have their own traditional system of self-governance confined to the village level administration only. The traditional village Chief called *Lal,* helped by a few other officials, virtually manages all the affairs of the village. The *Lal* has one principal assistant called Khawnbawl *Upa* and a few assistants called Khawnbawl. The *Lal* at first selects the *Khawnbawls* from among the adult male persons of the village in consultation with the village elders. Out of the selected *Khawnbawls* the *Lal* then selects the *Khawnbawl Upa* or his principal assistant. The traditional village council in a Hmar village, therefore, consists of the *Lal* (Chief), *Khawnbawl Upa* (principal assistant) and the *Khawnbawls* (assistants) and the male village elders. The *Lal* presides over the sittings of the village council and the council decides all matters connected with the village affairs.

The post of the *Lal* is hereditary while that of the others is not.

A Hmar village council basically serves the purpose of a village court. It tries all disputes and settles all disputes within the village. Unsettled disputes of grave nature are referred to the N.C. Hills District Council Court, Haflong.

For trying a case the plaintiff has to offer a pig to the members of the village council as a fee and such a fee in kind is called *Salam.* Although every member attending the trial session gets a share of the *Salam,* the *Lal,* however, gets the lion's share. Moreover, the plaintiff is also required to entertain the members of the village council with rice-beer prior to lending their ears to the complaints of the plaintiff.

In spite of the fact that the *Lal* exercises great powers, in practice he does not act like a dictator or autocrat. He gives sufficient weights to the opinions expressed by the other members of the village council.

In bygone days there was another village officer called *Tlangsam,* which means an announcer. The duty of the

Tlangsam was to proclaim the orders for the village Chief *Lal* among the people of the village. His other duties consisted of looking after the construction of the Chief's house, the bachelors' dormitory called *Bounzwal,* village street etc. In return for his services, he was exempted from doing any community labour.

However, this traditional official could not be traced in the Hmar villages situated within the territorial jurisdiction of the N.C. hills district. Now-a-days in a Hmar village, the *Lal* generally has a house of permanent nature with C.I. sheet roofs. Very often he is having a pucca house constructed by trained masons and carpenters. The *Bounzwal* or the bachelors' dormitory has already disappeared from the Hmar village of the North Cachar hills district. The construction of village streets is now done by the North Cachar Hills District Council through contractors. The *Tlangsam,* therefore, has no role to play now.

It is worthwhile to mention that the N.C. Hills District Council has not interfered with the affairs of the Hmar village councils. Wherever practically feasible, the *Lals* or the village Chiefs have been appointed by it as the village headman also. Thus a *Lal* in a Hmar village combines the traditional village headmanship with that of the District Council headmanship resulting in a synthesis.

Participation of Women

It is worthwhile to mention that in a traditional Hmar village council women are not assigned any role.

4. Traditional Self-Governing Institutions Among the Kukis of the North Cachar Hills District of Assam

The *Kukis* in Assam hills have 37 sub-groups. All the Kuki tribes except the *Rangkhols* are traditionally ruled by hereditary Chiefs. Each *Kuki* village has a hereditary Chief who possesses unlimited power and whose authority in the village is undisputed. In other words, he is supreme in his village. Although in each *Kuki* village there is a traditional village council also comprising all the adult male members of the village, nevertheless, it has practically no role to play since the Chief manages the village affairs single handed. He settles all the disputes in the village, selects the Jhum sites and decides when and where the village is to be moved. Each cultivator has to pay him a share of rice produced by him in the Jhum and the quantity depends on the quality of Jhum land allotted to him. The Chief also receives a portion of any animal killed by any villager of his village. Besides this, he also receives the entire amount of fines levied on the offenders.

But the Chief has some obligations also. He has to support the orphans and others who do not have any means of livelihood by providing food and shelter. In return, of course, they have to work for the Chief. Orphan girls brought up in Chief's house are released when they get married. It is also the Chief who receives the bride price in the event of such a marriage. The Chief has some petty officials to help him in discharging his duties and they are appointed by him and they would hold office only at his pleasure.

However, the most outstanding feature of the *Kuki* chieftainship is the fact that a *Kuki* Chief does not generally act like a dictator in spite of his unlimited powers.

However, the emergence of new leadership has now made the *Kuki* Chiefs somewhat powerless. Realising their importance, the *Kuki* Chiefs have been appointed as the village headmen by the N.C. Hill District Council.

In this institution of the Kuki society, the women have no role to play.

The *Rangkhols*, on the other hand, have a democratic tradition. Each *Rangkhol* village is administered by a group of officials selected by the village people. And as such the question of hereditary Chief of other *Kuki* tribes does not arise here. The traditional headman of a Rangkhol village is called *Kalim* and the assistant village headman is called *Kabur*. The *Kalim* has an assistant to help him in discharging his duties and he is called *Chapia-Kalim*. Similarly *Kabur* has also an assistant who is called *Chapia-Kabur*. All the posts mentioned above are open to all villagers. However an aspirant for the post of the village headmanship has to start at the bottom of the official hierchy.

The *Kalim* with the help of the other three officials tries cases, settles disputes, allots Jhum sites and maintains law and order in the village. If the people of a village are not satisfied with the work of a particular official, he may be removed from the office.

The women in the *Rangkhol* society, like the other *Kuki* tribes, have no role to play in the traditional self-governing institution.

5. Traditional Self-governing Institutions Among the Zemei Nagas of the North Cachar Hills District of Assam

In each *Zemei* village within the jurisdiction of the North Cachar Hills district there is a traditional village council called *Samkakibe* comprising all the adult male members of the village. This village council is headed by the traditional village headman who is called *Matai*. The other functionaries of the council are the *Kadepeo* or the land owner, the village priest called *Paitingko* and the assistant village headman called *Mataichepeo*.

The post of the village headman of a *Zemei* village is not hereditary. Similar is the case with the other two officials, namely the *Paitingko* and the *Mataichepeo*. The post of the *Kadepeo* is of course, hereditary.

The main functions of the village council of a *Zemei* village are to maintain law and order within the village, settle disputes arising out of land, property, theft, adultery, divorce, etc., select Jhum sites and allot Jhum plots among the different households of the village, decide the shifting of village to a new village site and also to approve the celebration of various community festivals.

Another important task assigned to the traditional *Zemei* village council is to guide the members of the *Hengseuki*, the dormitory of the boys and the members *Leuseuki*, the dormitory of the girls, in doing the welfare works in the village like construction of village roads and repairing of existing roads, bringing water to the village from the nearby hills through bamboo pipes, etc.

It is also important to note here that when the village council imposes fine on the person or persons, it is to be paid in kind only and generally it is in terms of domestic animals.

The cases settled by the village council are required to be referred to the North Cachar Hills District Council Court at Haflong.

Although *Matai*, the headman in a *Zemei* village, is also the head of the village council *Samkakibe*, nevertheless, the most influential member of the village council is the *Kadepeo*, the land owner. By virtue of being the landlord in the village, his decision is final and binding.

Like the other tribes, in the *Zemei* Naga traditional self-governing institutional set-up, women have no role to play.

An Assessment of the Self-Governing Institutions

From our above discussions on the traditional self-governing institutions among the hill tribal groups of Assam, the following few important facts have emerged:

1.1. Only among the five tribal communities inhabiting the hill areas of Assam the traditional self-governing institutions are still functioning.

1.2. Among all the five communities, namely, the Karbis, Dimasa Kacharis, Hmars, Kukis and Zemei Nagas the village councils headed by the village headmen have been discharging their duties without interference from the authorities of the District Councils.

1.3. In the North Cachar hills district there has been better co-ordination between the village councils and the District Council authorities in the sense that the traditional village headmen have been recognised as the District Council headmen also. Secondly, they have been assigned some important duties some of which are developmental in nature.

1.4. Among the Karbis of the Karbi Anglong district, apart from self-governing institutions at the village level there are two more traditional self-governing institutions at the regional and sub-regional levels. However, this three-tier traditional administration is now confined to the Hamren subdivision of the district only.

1.5. In most cases the functionaries of the traditional institutions are democratically selected by the people.

1.6. Women are completely deprived of participation in the affairs of traditional self-governing institutions. However, in the trial of cases where women are involved, the Dimasa Kacharis allow aged Dimasa women to participate in the sittings of the *Salis*. The same is the case with the Karbis also.

1.7. The traditional village councils have been performing three most important activities, viz., (1) maintenance of law and order, (2) trial of cases except those of grave nature and (3) disciplining and controlling the village youth.

1.8. It is also observed that the village councils have been extending their help and co-operation in implementing the rural development schemes including JRY in their concerned villages whenever such helps are sought for by the implementing authority, i.e., the authority of the development blocks.

1.9. For all practical purposes, the traditional village councils could be regarded as *Gaon Panchayats* without formal election of the members.

1.10. In the Karbi Anglong district some of the powers exercised by the traditional village council *Mei* have already been curtailed through legislation (Jhum Control Regulation).

11

Traditional Self-Governing Institutions of the Hill Tribes of Manipur: An Economist's View

– *Amar Yumnam*

Introduction

Homo sapiens, being social animals, have always needed a structure which provides them a social space to operate. This space needed to be regulated with a hierarchy for command and enforcement of norms. In other words, they have always needed an agency as means to protect and project their interests. In modern parlance, they needed a government with established and accepted norms of governance. In still other words, they have always needed a political power possessing the "Right of making Laws with Penalties of Death, and consequently all less Penalties, for the Regulating and Preserving of Property, and of employing the force of the Community, in the Execution of such Laws, and in the defence of the Common-wealth from Foreign Injury, and all this only for the Public Good." (Locke, <1689>, 1988, p. 268). Traditional self-governing institutions are those institutions which had served and have been serving the cause of the communities by ensuring continuation of life and property[1] through a system of

[1] Both life and property will not carry any meaning in the absence of assurance of continuation. Such an assurance can be established and provided only by an agency of governance bound by established and accepted norms.

guiding principles, organisational structures and governing procedures.

MANIPUR

Traditional self-governing institutions of the hill tribes of Manipur can as well be appreciated in the context of the above perspective. These institutions have been fundamentally village-based, with certain variations among them. Though from the modern perspective they were local level institutions, yet they were all institutions of state in their own right however limited the scale might have been. They all were characterised by strong bondages among the members though the linkages with the outside were limited.

Despite the variations among the institutions from village to village, they are generally grouped into two on the basis of commonality of features and groupings of the communities on the basis of origins. They are institutions of the Naga group of communities and those of the Kuki group of communities.

The variations between these two groups of communities are by now fairly generally known. Before we describe them, it would be more rewarding to examine the factors underlying the selection and establishment of a village and also the shifting to a new village. These factors were more or less common between the two groups.

Two factors had been of primary consideration in the selection of space for settlement and establishment of a village. One factor is economic and another strategic. The first economic consideration is the carrying capacity of the plot in space selected for settlement and establishment of a village. The plot should have the potential to yield agricultural output enough to ensure the continuity of life of the people. The second economic consideration is the easy availability of drinking water. Given the locational context of the hills, time and energy spent in fetching drinking water must have been a primary consideration in the selection of land for settlement. Besides, given the level of medical advancement of the earlier times, epidemics were a real menace. The economic cost of epidemics had been heavy on any group and necessarily availability of drinking water had to be a primary consideration in the selection of land for settlement.

The other significant consideration is the level of safety of the selected plot of land from the attacks of the enemy. As the level of development of the economy was still very primitive and basically subsistence oriented, external attacks could be very costly in real economic terms. This was particularly so as the degree of commercialisation was practically low, if any. In these circumstances, it was imperative that a plot was selected for its potential of easy defence against primitive accumulators. This condition naturally impacted upon the institutional character of any village[2]. The common destiny of collective unity and survival had necessarily to be accepted and shared. This explains the prevalence of high level of social capital and social cohesiveness among the various tribal communities.

The above considerations were equally valid in the selection of a new village and shifting there. However, the additional factors prompting shifting to a new village are overpopulation, frequency of conflicts, scarcity of drinking water and spread of epidemic. The technological intensity of farming was low, and, *ipso facto,* extensive cultivation was the primary means for procuring higher output. With the rise in population and the concomitant requirement for additional agricultural output, extensive cultivation became increasingly infeasible economically. First, the additional land areas immediately available for extensive cultivation were not suitable for the type of farming in practice.

---

[2] The institution of Boys'/Bachelors' Dormitory was an early version of organised army.

Secondly, supervision could be very costly both in terms of life and economics. So it was always more economical for a group[3] to shift out to a new village. Incompatibility of preferences with the ruling group could also be another reason for a group to shift out to a new village. Considerations relating to water and epidemic have already been explained.

Self-Governing Institutions

Having understood the underlying considerations governing the selection of a piece of land for establishment of a village, we can now describe the self-governing institutions. The above exercise has been deliberate in the sense that the functional roles of these institutions were primarily determined by the considerations governing the establishment of villages.

A village would generally consist of two or more clans. A village of either the Naga or the Kuki would have a Chief, generally known as Khunpu or Khullakpa under the influence of the Meetei monarchs. The major difference lies in how far the wishes of the Chief prevailed.

Among the Naga group of village communities, it is basically the Village Chief-in-Council which governs. This consists of village elders who would jointly decide on village issues. Though there is no separate office for the Village Chief-in-Council, it is generally attached to the house of a respectable elder person[4] of the village. The Council would decide on programmes of the village both at times of peace and war. It looks after the requirements of defence, footpaths and drinking water, etc. These are the executive functions of the Council. It would also decide on customs and traditions, and thereby performing the legislative part of governance. It would also administer justice.

---

[3] The group should however have the potential to grow through reproduction and the capacity to protect itself from dangers.

[4] Invariably male.

Among the Kuki group of villages, it is the Chief who decides on executive, legislative and judicial matters. He is expected to be strong physically and morally, possess a strong sense of justice and alive to the genuine issues of the community in the village. He is also expected to take the village elders into confidence while deciding on critical issues.

The predominance of elders in both the systems needs an explanation. In a world where the rate of economic change was slow, survival was on the brink of subsistence, and inter-linkages with the outside were both unreliable and mostly nonexistent, the only assured means for the continuation of human life was the one tested through time and space. And who would have a better knowledge of this means than the elders of a village? There would be elders who would each be experts in general administration, defence, agriculture, animal husbandry, etc.

Evolutionary Challenges

The fundamental orientation of the traditional self-governing institutions, as mentioned above, was continuation of life and property. They were not designed for fostering change and transformation. Another fundamental orientation was the creation and maintenance of a strong internal bondage within the village. The village and the institution governing the village was neither designed nor destined for erecting and enhancing bridges with the world outside. On the other hand, modern developmental interventions are not designed to build on traditional social cohesion and social capital. This contradiction has certainly given a body blow to the relevance and functional use of the traditional self-governing institutions.

Secondly, the traditional functional role of ensuring safety has become irrelevant and meaningless. First, the role of a defender has now been undertaken by the modern state on a much larger and meaningful scale. Secondly, even on the traditional limited scale, the meaning of defending against enemy attacks bears no meaning in the context of AK-47s.

Thirdly, in the traditional social, executive, legislative and judicial roles too, the traditional institutions have now been replaced by the modern state.[5]

The Dilemma and the Tragedy

The dilemma facing these traditional institutions is that they are not being allowed to enjoy the fate of death as antiquated forms of governance and facilitate the emergence of better forms. Further, these are not being allowed to independently play whatever little role they could in the social space. These have, however, become convenient institutions for conveying and imposing the wishes of groups who have wielded the power to prevail their wishes over others. This has had the tragic effect of stunting the emergence and growth of democratic values among the general populace. It is a case of neither here nor there.

Reference

Locke, John, *Two Treatises of Government,* edited by Peter Laslett, Cambridge texts in the history of political thought, Cambridge University Press, 1988.

[5] The effectiveness of the delivery is altogether a different question.

Index

❑❑❑